UNLOCKING
the
Treasure

A Bible Study for Moms
Entrusted with Special-
Needs Children

Bev Roozeboom

WestBow
PRESS
A DIVISION OF THOMAS NELSON

All Scripture quotations, unless otherwise indicated, are taken from the Holy Bible, New International Version®. NIV®. Copyright © 1973, 1978, 1984 by International Bible Society. Used by permission of Zondervan. All rights reserved.

Scripture quotations marked CEV are from the Contemporary English Version. Copyright 1991, 1992, 1995 American Bible Society. Used by permission.

Scripture quotations marked MSG are taken from The Message. Copyright 1993, 1994, 1995, 1996, 2000, 2001, 2002. Used by permission of NavPress.

Scripture quotations marked AMP are taken from the Amplified Bible. Copyright 1954, 1958, 1962, 1964, 1965, 1987 by the Lockman Foundation. Used by permission.

Scripture quotations marked NCV are taken from the New Century Version. Copyright 2005 by Thomas Nelson, Inc. Used by permission. All rights reserved.

Scripture quotations marked HCSB are taken from the Holman Christian Standard Bible. Copyright 2003, 2002, 2000, 1999 by Holman Bible Publishers. All rights reserved.

Scripture quotations marked NLT are taken from the Holy Bible, New Living Translation, copyright 1996, 2004, 2007 by Tyndale House Foundation. Used by permission of Tyndale House Publishers, Inc., Carol Stream, Illinois 60188. All rights reserved.

WestBow Press books may be ordered through booksellers or by contacting:

WestBow Press
A Division of Thomas Nelson
1663 Liberty Drive
Bloomington, IN 47403
www.westbowpress.com
1-(866) 928-1240

Because of the dynamic nature of the Internet, any web addresses or links contained in this book may have changed since publication and may no longer be valid. The views expressed in this work are solely those of the author and do not necessarily reflect the views of the publisher, and the publisher hereby disclaims any responsibility for them.

Any people depicted in stock imagery provided by Thinkstock are models, and such images are being used for illustrative purposes only.

Certain stock imagery © Thinkstock.

ISBN: 978-1-4497-1599-1 (sc)
ISBN: 978-1-4497-1598-4 (e)

Library of Congress Control Number: 2011927124

Printed in the United States of America

WestBow Press rev. date: 5/18/2011

TABLE OF CONTENTS

PREFACE

I'm so glad you dared to peak between the covers of this study book! If you are a mom of a child with special needs—or the mom of a very difficult child—then you are a woman dealing with challenges far greater than you ever imagined. Perhaps you struggle because you feel no one really understands your pain. Maybe you're weary of well-meaning people telling you that God won't give you more than you can handle. Perhaps you're secretly wondering if God has forgotten you, or worse yet, that He's punishing you for some past sin. Deep in your heart you may be angry with God, wondering why He chose *you* to have a child with "special" needs.

I understand. I've been where you are. I *am* where you are. My husband and I have a teenage son who has struggled with mental illness and learning disabilities since early childhood. When we adopted our son as an infant, we knew he had special needs, and we assumed we would encounter bumps and endure bruises along the way. We thought we were well aware of and well prepared for any challenges we would encounter.

We soon realized, however, that we had been plunged into a reality in which we had little control and limited knowledge. We didn't know anything about childhood mental illness, much less how to parent a child with such a diagnosis. For years we floundered, trying to find a knowledgeable psychiatrist, get a correct diagnosis, determine the best medications, find a decent therapist, and come up with some effective techniques for managing behavior. Along the way, we struggled with family issues, school issues, and church issues. We frequently felt isolated in our struggle. As we wrestled with these concerns, we often asked ourselves, "Where is God in all of this? What is His plan? What larger purpose did God have in mind when He chose us to love and care for this precious child?"

I invite you to join me on a journey that will take us to the heart of God. God has so much He wants us to learn about Him! He wants to set us free from trying to make life fit *our* ideal, so that we may enjoy the abundant life He has prepared for us. As we search His Word and discover His unfailing promises, we will uncover precious treasures. Like opening a nesting doll, our search will bring to light one treasure after another—each one uniquely beautiful and precious—designed with you in mind!

"He will be the sure foundation for your times, a rich store of salvation and wisdom and knowledge; the fear of the Lord is the key to this treasure." (Is. 33:6)

God has treasures prepared for us that our minds cannot even begin to conceive! Let's unlock His Word and open it together to see what God wants to reveal to us—about ourselves, about the journey we're on, and ultimately about *Him!*

Bev Roozeboom

INTRODUCTORY LESSON

Finding Hope in His Promises

To complete together as a group at the first lesson.

THE LORD IS FAITHFUL
TO HIS PROMISES...

I'm so thankful you decided to come along on this journey to unlock God's priceless treasure! My prayer is that you are in a group with several other moms who also have children with special needs. Once a week you can join together to discuss the lessons you completed during the week. This introductory lesson is intended for you to work on together as a group. It will launch you into the next five weeks of individual study. If you were unable to form a study group, you will be able to complete this Bible study on your own.

As we work through this introductory lesson, we will focus our attention on several of God's promises. Together we will discover that God has boldly made some amazing promises to us, and that He *always* keeps His promises—each and every one!

Part 1: God's Promises...

Complete this section together as a group

Ps. 145:8–9; 13–20: "The Lord is gracious and compassionate, slow to anger and rich in love. 9 The Lord is good to all; He has compassion on all He has made.... 13 Your kingdom is an everlasting kingdom, and Your dominion endures through all generations. The Lord is faithful to all His promises and loving toward all He has made. 14 The Lord upholds all those who fall and lifts up all who are bowed down. 15 The eyes of all look to You, and You give them their food at the proper time. 16 You open Your hand and satisfy the desires of every living thing. 17 The Lord is righteous in all His ways and loving toward all He has made. 18 The Lord is near to all who call on Him, to all who call on Him in truth. 19 He fulfills the desires of those who fear him; He hears their cry and saves them. 20 The Lord watches over all who love Him, but all the wicked He will destroy."

Read verses 8 and 9.

1. How is the Lord defined in these verses?

2. On whom does the Lord have compassion?

Dictionary.com defines compassion as "A feeling of deep sympathy and sorrow for another who is stricken by misfortune, accompanied by a strong desire to alleviate the suffering."[1] *Strong's Exhaustive Concordance of the Bible* explains, "Feelings of compassion are usually accompanied by acts of compassion."[2]

3. When do we *feel* compassion towards others?

4. How do we *show* compassion to others?

5. When it became evident that your child had special needs, did anyone act compassionately towards you? What were some specific ways that people showed you compassion?

6. Did you sense *God* acting compassionately towards you? If so, how? If not, what makes you say this?

Did you realize that the Hebrew word for *compassion* has the same root as the word for *womb?*

7. List several functions of the womb.

8. What does this connection with the womb tell you about God's compassion?

This is how God expresses His compassion! When we are wrapped and embraced in Him, we lack nothing. He provides for all of our needs. He nurtures us and carries us. We are safe and secure.

9. In what ways do you feel the Lord's compassion surrounding you today?

Read verses 13 through 20.

10. How many promises does God keep?

11. Circle the word "all" each time it appears in these verses. What does this repetition tell you?

We're told in verse 13 that the Lord is *faithful.*

12. How would you define "faithful"?

In place of the word *faithful,* other versions of the Bible use words such as *gracious and kind.* Still other translations say that the Lord *keeps His word and does everything He says.*

13. Will God *ever* break a promise He's made to us?

14. Which promise listed in these verses means the most to you at this time in your life? Why?

---

1   *Dictionary.com Unabridged*, (Random House, Inc. 08 Mar. 2011), <Dictionary.com http://dictionary.reference. com/browse/compassion>.

2   James Strong, *Strong's Exhaustive Concordance of the Bible Larger Print Edition,* (Zondervan, 2001), 1957.

15. Re-read verse 18. To whom is the Lord near?

16. What do you think it means to "call on Him in truth"?

Listen to how verse 18 is written in these versions of the Bible.

- (Contemporary English Version) "…and you are near to everyone whose prayers are sincere."

- (The Message—paraphrase) "God's there, listening for all who pray, for all who pray and mean it."

- (Amplified Bible) "The Lord is near to all who call upon Him, to all who call upon Him sincerely and in truth."

- (New Century Version) "The Lord is close to everyone who prays to him, to all who truly pray to him."

- (Holman Christian Standard Bible) "The LORD is near all who call out to Him, all who call out to Him with integrity."

17. Let's take another close look at our passage. Each time you come across descriptions of the Lord's identity and the promises He has made, please fill in the blanks.

v. 8   The Lord is _____ and _____

v. 8   (The Lord is)_____ to anger and _____ in love

v. 9   The Lord is _____

v. 9   He has _____

v. 13 Your kingdom is _____

v. 13 Your dominion _____

v. 13 The Lord is _____

v. 13 (The Lord is) _____

v. 14 The Lord _____

v. 14 (The Lord) _____ _____

v. 15 You _____

v. 16 You _____ Your hand

v. 16 (You) _____ the desires

v. 17 The Lord is _____

v. 17 (The Lord is) _____

v. 18 The Lord is _____

v. 19 He _____ the desires

v. 19 He _____

v. 19 (He) _____

v. 20 The Lord _____

v. 20 He will _____ (the wicked)

Wow! So many promises packed into ten verses! Imagine how many more promises the treasure of God's Word must contain! Over the next five weeks, we will look closely at some of these promises. As we unlock this treasure, we will uncover some amazing truths. Most importantly, we will discover God's intimate love for us!

Our God is an available God! He is **always near** when we sincerely seek Him. The Lord promises to faithfully lift us up when our shoulders are weighed down with burdens. He promises to satisfy and fulfill our desires. He reassures us that He hears our cries and will save us. He is a loving, compassionate, and righteous Father!

Part 2: How do we *know* God will keep His promises?

His Word tells us!

For personal reflection

Spend ten to fifteen minutes alone, quietly reading the following verses. Then answer the three questions that follow. Your responses are only for your personal reflection; you do not need to share them with the group.

- Num. 23:19: "God is not a man, that He should lie, nor a son of man, that He should change His mind. Does He speak and then not act? Does He promise and not fulfill?"

- 1 Sam. 15:29: "He who is the Glory of Israel does not lie or change His mind; for He is not a man, that He should change His mind."

- Josh. 21:45: "Not one of all the Lord's good promises to the house of Israel failed; every one was fulfilled."

- Ps. 119:50: "My comfort in my suffering is this; Your promise has given me life."

- James 1:17: "Every good and perfect gift is from above, coming down from the Father of the heavenly lights, who does not change like shifting shadows."

- 2 Cor. 1:20-22 (NLT): "For all of God's promises have been fulfilled in Christ with a resounding 'Yes!' And through Christ, our 'Amen' (which means 'Yes') ascends to God for His glory. 21 Now it is God who makes both us and you stand firm in Christ. He anointed us, 22 set His seal of ownership on us, and put His Spirit in our hearts as a deposit, guaranteeing what is to come."

1. Meditate on these verses. What theme is consistent in all of them?

2. Write down what you sense the Lord is saying to you.

3. Reread 2 Corinthians 1:20–22 and spend a few minutes meditating on this passage. What message does the Lord have for you in these verses?

God's promises are "yes" in Christ. In other words, Jesus, in His humanity, fulfilled the promises God made regarding the Messiah. What was Jesus the Messiah like? How did He treat the people with whom He walked and who daily received His ministry? In the gospels we see that Jesus treated people with love, mercy, compassion, healing, gentleness, and grace. Do you believe that Jesus treats us this way today? He does! James 1:17 reminds us that God does not change.

We're told in 2 Cor. 1:20-22 that God has anointed us, claimed us as His own, and even poured out His Spirit into our hearts! Do you believe this is true for *you*? If you're a believer, perhaps you don't question the fact that God "set His seal of ownership on you and put His Spirit in your heart." But what about the "anointed" part? Do you believe God has anointed you? What does this even mean? How can God's anointing help us with our daily struggles?

As we go through this study together, we will dig more deeply into this. We will discover the love, power, and anointing God has given us. We will see that He has equipped us with everything we need for the life He's called us to live.

Along with the Psalmist, we'll be able to say, "My comfort in my suffering is this; Your promise has given me life" (Ps. 119:50) We can do it, sisters! "The Lord is faithful to all of His promises and loving toward all He has made" (Ps. 145:13b).

Part 3: Wrapping it up…

Finish the session together as a group

"The Lord is near to all who call on Him, to all who call on Him in truth." (Ps. 145:18)

How can others be in prayer for you this week? How can you pray for others?

Go around the table and share prayer requests. Remember your commitment to keep this group as a safe place and to hold your conversations in confidence. What you share in the privacy of this group will stay here. After individuals have made requests, either have one person pray through the requests or have a time of "popcorn" prayer.

*Parts One and Three should be completed together as a group. Part Two is intended for individual reflection and will not be discussed in the group. Allow ten minutes to complete Part Two.

WEEK 1

His Unfailing Love

"How great is the love the Father has lavished on us, that we should be called children of God! And that is what we are!"—1 John 3:1

Our introductory lesson reminded us that God always keeps His promises. Throughout the next five weeks, we will more fully explore some of these promises. We will also hear reminders that God has *not* promised us a life of ease. While all moms face this reality from time to time, we face it daily.

As believers, we know that someday—in the new heaven and new earth—God will remove all pain, sorrow, tears, grief, and imperfections. Life will be as God originally intended it. Everything will be renewed and restored to perfection. But what about *today?* What promises can I hold onto for today? After all, *today* I'm faced with a raging, aggressive teenager who struggles with a mental illness. My friend is exhausted with her sweet little boy who has physical and intellectual disabilities. Another friend worries about her child's future. Her precious daughter suddenly became ill with a rare infection and now faces limitations she had not previously encountered.

I know what God has promised me when I die, but what are His promises for me *today?* In John 10:10, Jesus tells us, "The thief [Satan] comes only to steal and kill and destroy; I have come that you may have life, and have it to the full." The Amplified Bible reads this way: "The thief comes only in order to steal and kill and destroy. I came that you may have and enjoy life, and have it in abundance (to the full, till it overflows)." I love that! Jesus promises us that we can enjoy an abundant life right now!

My prayer as we go on this journey is that we'll be given a fresh awareness of God's love. I pray that together we'll discover ways to enjoy a full and abundant life on this earth, even in the midst of daily struggles and challenges. God has not given us these children to punish us. Their lives were not an accident; they are not an anomaly in God's eyes. In His perfect wisdom, He chose to give us the children He did. God knew the route would be difficult, but He's given us an excellent guidebook. God has placed a challenging and oftentimes wearisome calling before us, but He's equipped us for the task! Let's do it together!

This study includes five daily lessons for each week. The lessons are purposefully short and will not take long to complete. The Scripture passages appear in each daily reading, so you won't even have to hunt down your Bible! The passages come from the New International Version, unless otherwise noted. I would encourage you to spend a few minutes each day on the lessons so that the truths will sink deeply into the nooks and crannies of your life.

Each day you will discover several personal application questions to help you apply God's Word to your individual situation. I would encourage you to answer these questions honestly. For too long, many of us have draped a blanket over our true emotions. We've worried that others would not understand the challenges with which we're dealing and would judge us unfairly. But in this study it's okay to be intensely honest! Let's be open with ourselves, with others, and most importantly with God. You will also find some personal reflection questions scattered throughout the study. These are meant to be just between you and God. Again, I would encourage you to open your heart in honesty. Give Him your pain and allow Him to begin to work His healing in your life.

Finally, a short reading entitled, "Walking the Journey," will follow each day's lesson. Most of these entries are real-life stories from moms like you and me—moms on this journey called "special needs."

Let's get started unlocking God's treasure…beginning with His lavish love!

Week 1, Day 1

God's Lavish Love

Please read each passage. Ask God to open the eyes of your heart so that you will understand what He is saying to you.

1. 1 John 3:1: "How great is the love the Father has lavished on us, that we should be called children of God! And that is what we are!"

    A. Who are we to God?

    B. What word or phrase in this verse is especially meaningful to you? Why?

2. Zeph. 3:17: "The Lord your God is with you, He is mighty to save. He will take great delight in you, He will quiet you with His love, He will rejoice over you with singing."

    A. In this verse, how is God depicted?

    _____ A stern judge

    _____ A grumpy old man

    _____ A gentle, loving parent

    _____ A cold, distant ruler

    B. What is God's message for you in this verse? What does He want you to know?

3. Ps. 42:8: "By day the Lord directs His love, at night His song is within me—a prayer to the God of my life."

    Ps. 143:8 "Let the morning bring me word of Your unfailing love, for I have put my trust in You."

    Ps. 55:17 "Evening, morning and noon I cry out in distress, and he hears my voice."

    Ps. 92:2 "It is good…to proclaim Your unfailing love in the morning, Your faithfulness in the evening."

Ps. 59:16 "But I will sing of Your strength, in the morning I will sing of Your love; for You are my fortress, my refuge in times of trouble."

A. Is there ever a time God is not directing His love towards us? In the verses above, circle all the references to time of day. After you have completed that, underline the phrases that describe God's love for us.

B. When you are having a bad day, how can God be a fortress and a refuge? (See Psalm 59:16.)

C. Reflect on the past twenty-four hours of your life. In what tangible ways did God show you His love?

D. What evidence do you have in your life of the Lord's unfailing love?

Psalm 23 is a favorite passage to many. Verse six contains an incredible promise. Listen to how the New Living Translation presents it: "Surely Your goodness and unfailing love will pursue me all the days of my life, and I will live in the house of the Lord forever." Have you ever thought of God's love *pursuing* you? To "pursue" means to "follow close upon; to chase after." God is not content to just say He loves us. No, He follows closely on our heels, reminding us morning, noon, and night of His unfailing love. Are you listening?

4. How did the Lord speak to you today?

WALKING THE JOURNEY

Today my heart melted....

I was having a rough day, and I just so happened to be listening to the first song on our blog playlist, "Beautiful," by Shawn McDonald. This song has been special to me since the days when my husband and I were dating, but it now holds an even deeper place in my heart. As I listened to this song, I was sitting right across from Cayla on the floor and belting out the words while looking into her eyes. I was tearing up just thinking about how these words mean so much more now that we have our little Cayla Joy.

In one stretch, the lyrics say:

What a beautiful God

And what am I, that I might be called Your child

What am I, what am I, that You might know me, my King

Beautiful colors all around me, oh

Painted all over the sky

The same hands that created all of this

They created you and I

What a beautiful God.[3]

Yes, our little miracle from above is *beautiful* and created *just* as God wanted her to be! And as if this were not already enough, Cayla just looked at me and began clapping. She did this several times throughout the song—with no prompting. It was as if she completely understood and was enjoying watching me begin to understand how God's plan is unfolding for her life, for all of our lives. She is our special little angel and a touch of Heaven here on earth. God knows best, even when we begin to question him....

Leah's baby daughter, Cayla, has Down syndrome. This was posted on her blog, http://littlegarland. blogspot.com. Used with permission.

---

3   Shawn Mc Donald, *Beautiful,* Simply Nothing, 2004

WEEK 1, DAY 2

GOD'S GENTLE COMPASSION

As we focus on God's compassion today, remember what we learned in our introductory lesson. The Hebrew word for *compassion* has the same root as the Hebrew word for *womb*. What a tender picture of how God touches us in His compassion!

Please read each passage. Ask God to open the eyes of your heart so that you will understand what He is saying to you.

1. Is. 40:11: "He tends His flock like a Shepherd; He gathers the lambs in His arms and carries them close to His heart; He gently leads those that have young."

    A. Who is the Shepherd?

    B. Who is the Shepherd caring for? (Give two answers)

        1.

        2.

    C. Where does the Shepherd hold the lambs?

    D. How does the Shepherd care for "those that have young"?

    What a beautiful description of how God takes care of moms and their children. Do you ever think He's forgotten about you or your child? Do you ever wonder if He's left you all alone to flounder? How comforting to know that the Good Shepherd is constantly holding the most defenseless members of society close to His heart. What a gentle reminder that His compassionate love extends to those of us who parent these precious children.

2. Lam. 3:22–24: "Because of the Lord's great love we are not consumed, for His compassions never fail. They are new every morning; great is Your faithfulness. I say to myself, 'The Lord is my portion; therefore I will wait for Him.'"

    A. What struggles tend to "consume" you in your day-to-day living?

    B. What do these verses tell us about the Lord's compassion?

C. When you're feeling consumed by the demands of the day—when your child is sucking all your energy and you're exhausted and frustrated—how can this passage be a comfort to you?

3. Jer. 31:3: "The Lord appeared to us in the past saying: 'I have loved you with an everlasting love; I have drawn you with loving kindness.'"

The New Living Translation presents this verse a little differently: "Long ago the Lord said to Israel: 'I have loved you, my people, with an everlasting love. With unfailing love I have drawn you to myself.'"

The Hebrew word for love used in the first part of this verse is *ahab.* This is how Mary Kassian, in her book, *Knowing God by Name,* describes *ahab.* "This word is used in the Old Testament to describe strong affection for someone based on relationship…The Lord delights in us and is inclined toward us. He desires us with affectionate (*ahab)* love." [4]

The second reference to love in this verse ("loving-kindness," "everlasting love," "unfailing love") uses the Hebrew word *chesed.* "*Chesed* speaks of a love that is firmly rooted in God's character. It involves loyalty, steadfastness, and covenant commitment as well as kindness, tenderness, and mercy…. It's a love that doesn't depend on the response or behavior of the receiver, but rather on the steadfast character and commitment of the giver." [5]

A. Write about a time from your past that reminds you that God has always loved you, even when you were a little girl (perhaps even before you knew Him). (*This is a personal reflection question. You will not be asked to share this in the group.*)

B. What motivates God's kindness and compassion for us?

The word *everlasting* means "forever; from eternity; from old, ancient, lasting; for a duration." [6] In other words, God's love for us began even before we were born and it will continue forever!

4. How did the Lord speak to you today?

---

4   Mary A. Kassian, *Knowing God by Name: A Personal Encounter* (Nashville: LifeWay Press, 2008), 39.

5   Ibid.

6   James Strong, *The Strongest Strong's Exhaustive Concordance of the Bible Larger Print Edition* (Zondervan, 2001), 1927.

WALKING THE JOURNEY

Kyle has been so unstable the past several days. Last night I was up with him from 3:30–5:30 a.m. As I was watching his rapidly shifting moods, a verse from Jeremiah kept running through my mind. I felt the arms of God holding me close and heard His voice gently whisper to my heart, "I have loved you with an everlasting love; I have drawn you with loving-kindness." Wrapped in His arms, I got through the night.

An entry from my personal journal when our son was eleven years old.

WEEK 1, DAY 3

JESUS' LOVE FOR CHILDREN

On Day One we immersed ourselves in God's lavish and unfailing love. Yesterday we focused on God's tender compassion. Today we're going to uncover some passages that remind us how deeply the Lord loves His precious children.

Please read each passage. Ask God to open the eyes of your heart so that you will understand what He is saying to you.

1. Matt. 18:1–5: "At that time the disciples came to Jesus and asked, 'Who is the greatest in the kingdom of heaven?' He called a little child and had him stand among them. And he said: 'I tell you the truth, unless you change and become like little children, you will never enter the kingdom of heaven. Therefore, whoever humbles himself like this child is the greatest in the kingdom of heaven. And whoever welcomes a little child like this in my name welcomes me.'"

   A. What question did Jesus' disciples ask?

   B. What (who) did Jesus use as an object lesson to teach His disciples?

   C. How did Jesus answer them? Fill in the blanks. "…He said: 'I tell you the truth, unless you _____ and become like _____ _____, you will never enter the kingdom of heaven. Therefore, whoever _____ himself like this child is the greatest in the kingdom of heaven. And whoever _____ a little child like this in _____ _____ welcomes me.'"

   D. When Jesus told his disciples that they must "change and become like little children," what do you think He meant?

2. The same incident was also recorded in Mark 9:36–37. This version comes from The Message: "He [Jesus] put a child in the middle of the room. Then, cradling the little one in his arms, he said, 'Whoever embraces one of these children as I do, embraces me, and far more than me—God who sent me.'"

   A. Close your eyes for a moment and picture this scene. Place yourself in the room with Jesus and the children. What do you see on Jesus' face? What does His voice sound like? How does the little child feel? Write about your thoughts.

B. Now picture *your own child* in Jesus' arms. What emotions are evident in Jesus? How does your child react to Him? How does this touch your heart?

C. Now picture *yourself* in Jesus' arms. What are your emotions? What is Jesus tenderly whispering to you?

3. Matt. 18:10: "Beware that you do not despise or feel scornful toward or think little of one of these little ones, for I tell you that in heaven their angels always are in the presence of and look upon the face of My Father who is in heaven." (AMP)

In this section, Jesus continues to teach His disciples about true greatness. Once again He refers to a little child.

A. What caution does Jesus give His disciples in Matthew 18:10?

B. Who do these "little ones" have watching over them?

I believe Jesus intends, in this saying, to include children of all ages who are forever "childlike" in their intellect, emotions, actions, and physical functions. Wouldn't it be just like our loving Father to handpick specific guardian angels to watch over our children with special needs? Moms, we're not doing this alone! We have the Holy Spirit living within us—guiding, directing, and comforting. We also have angels surrounding our children and us—protecting, serving, and ministering.

C. Reread Matthew 18:10. In whose presence do the children's angels always abide?

D. What reassurance does this give you?

4. How did the Lord speak to you today?

WALKING THE JOURNEY

I have been struggling some with this disease being Anna's lot in life. I am thankful that God spared her life, but yet what I really want for her is to be the way she was before. Sometimes it is very hard to understand why God answered some prayers, but not others. I do believe He could have spared her all of this, but He allowed it. I have seen enough of God working that I don't really doubt His existence, but sometimes I find myself doubting His goodness. I really struggle with that. In my heart of hearts, I know He is good and He loves Anna more than I ever could and that He has a plan for her life. I know He can use all of this for good.

But sometimes I have a hard time justifying all of that with what she will face throughout her life. I once heard someone talk about praying that God would allow your children to go through whatever they needed to in order to become the people He wants them to be. That made a big impression on me, and I have often prayed that for my kids. But now I want to just change my mind and say this is not what I meant. God gives us many promises in His word, but He never promises an easy road. Sometimes I just wish that He would.

God has continued to show me His way. Shortly after we got home, I was struggling with feeling that God really screwed up, and He just showed me that Satan was putting thoughts into my head. I really feel that Satan has been trying to convince me to change what I know of God's character. I just keep praying that God will show me some of what He is doing, but I know I need to trust Him even if He chooses not to show me.

I guess this got kind of heavy, but I have been feeling like I needed to be honest about my thoughts and feelings. Some people seem to think that going through something like this automatically makes me a saint, but I am not. I have doubts, frustration, and anger like everyone. I just try to trust God's love for me. Because that is what it all comes down to. If I know He loves me (and Anna), then I know I can trust Him.

Entry from a friend's Care Page update…

Julie's thoughts as she was in the hospital dealing with the sudden and severe illness of her young daughter—an illness which left her little girl permanently disabled.

Week 1, Day 4

Love Lessons from Job

Today we will look closely at the familiar story of Job. Possibly no one in all of Scripture, other than Jesus Christ, suffered as much as Job. Let's see what God wants to teach us about love from the life of Job.

Please read each passage. Ask God to open the eyes of your heart so that you will understand what He is saying to you.

1. Job 1:1–5, NLT: "There once was a man named Job who lived in the land of Uz. He was blameless—a man of complete integrity. He feared God and stayed away from evil. 2 He had seven sons and three daughters. 3 He owned 7,000 sheep, 3,000 camels, 500 teams of oxen, and 500 female donkeys. He also had many servants. He was, in fact, the richest person in that entire area. 4 Job's sons would take turns preparing feasts in their homes, and they would also invite their three sisters to celebrate with them. 5 When these celebrations ended—sometimes after several days—Job would purify his children. He would get up early in the morning and offer a burnt offering for each of them. For Job said to himself, 'Perhaps my children have sinned and have cursed God in their hearts.' This was Job's regular practice."

   A. What kind of man was Job?

   B. What was Job's "regular practice" (See verse 5.)?

   Let's take a close look at Job's life—at his blessings and his losses. Satan set out to destroy Job. Over time, God allowed Satan to kill Job's servants, animals, and even all of his children. Eventually Satan took Job's health as well. What was Job's response? "Naked I came from my mother's womb, and naked I will depart. The Lord gave and the Lord has taken away; may the name of the Lord be praised" (Job 1:21).

   C. What are some blessings the Lord has given you?

   D. What has the Lord withheld from you or even allowed to be taken from you?

   Job's friends were certain that he must have committed a terrible sin and that these calamities were his punishment.

E. Have you ever thought that perhaps your child's difficulties were your punishment for a past sin? *(This is a personal reflection question. You won't be asked to share this in your group.)*

Job's own wife scoffed at him for holding onto his integrity. She told him to "curse God and die." Job replied, "You are talking like a foolish woman. Shall we accept good from God, not trouble?" (Job 2:9–10). Job could accept that suffering and trials were part of life. But Job's biggest struggle was with not knowing *why* all of these calamities struck him. He was sure he hadn't done anything to warrant such serious punishment, despite his friends suggesting this as an explanation. As he agonized over his situation and listened to his friends, he found no comfort and received no answers. But even in his intense pain, Job found the resolve to testify that God was faithful. Job told his friends, "If I go to the east, He is not there; if I go to the west, I do not find Him. When He turns to the south, I catch no glimpse of Him. *But He knows the way that I take;* when He has tested me I will come forth as gold" (Job 23:8–10, italics mine). In other words, Job told his friends that even though he could not see God, God saw him. He was not lost to God!

Ultimately, when God replied to Job (Job 38–41), He didn't offer neat and tidy explanations. Instead He pointed to *Himself.* He reminded Job that *He is God.* In His Godhood, He is omniscient (all-knowing), omnipotent (all-powerful), and omnipresent (all-present). God told Job that it was better for him to *know God* than to know the answers.

Job finally learned that even though he had endured immeasurable loss, he had enough because he had God. Regardless of what we endure, we can be assured that God is enough for our lives and our future. Then, as in Job 19:25–27, we can declare with Job, "I know that my Redeemer lives, and that in the end He will stand upon the earth. And after my skin has been destroyed, yet in my flesh I will see God; I myself will see Him with my own eyes—I and not another. How my heart yearns within me!"

F. *(This is a personal reflection question. You will not need to share this with your group.)* Do you believe that *God is enough*? Do you desire a relationship with God more than anything else in life, even more than a healthy child, a satisfying marriage, or material blessings? If not, ask God to give you a deep desire and yearning for Him. Speak out loud Job's prayer of praise and desire from Job 19:25–27: "I know that my Redeemer lives, and that in the end He will stand upon the earth. And after my skin has been destroyed, yet in my flesh I will see God; I myself will see Him with my own eyes—I and not another. How my heart yearns within me!"

2. John 9:1–3: "As [Jesus] went along, He saw a man blind from birth. His disciples asked Him, 'Rabbi, who sinned, this man or his parents, that he was born blind?' 'Neither this man nor his parents sinned,' said Jesus, 'but this happened so that the work of God might be displayed in his life.'"

A. What assumption did the disciples make about the blind man and his parents?

B. How did Jesus answer the disciples?

In the verses following this encounter, we see that Jesus healed the blind man and fully restored his sight. When we witness complete healing, we can easily see "the work of God displayed." But what about when God answers prayers for physical, mental, or emotional healing with a "no"? Can we still say, along with Jesus, "This happened so that the work of God might be displayed in his or her life"?

C. How have you seen the work of God displayed in your child's life?

3. How did the Lord speak to you today?

WALKING THE JOURNEY

Does our suffering always result directly from personal sin? No. Through the life of Job we see that there are times we simply do not know why God allows certain pain and suffering to come into our lives. But what we can know for certain is that *God is good*. He is a loving, kind, merciful, patient, and immensely personal God. God is in control of this world—and our lives—and we can trust Him. In times of deep pain it's good to rehearse what the Bible tells us about God. Psalm 103 is a wonderful place to start!

The LORD is merciful! He is kind and patient, and His love never fails.

The LORD won't always be angry and point out our sins;

He doesn't punish us as our sins deserve.

How great is God's love for all who worship Him?

Greater than the distance between heaven and earth!

How far has the LORD taken our sins from us?

Farther than the distance from east to west!

Just as parents are kind to their children,

the LORD is kind to all who worship Him,

because He knows we are made of dust.

The LORD is always kind to those who worship Him,

and He keeps his promises to their descendants.

Ps. 103:8–14,17 (CEV)

Week 1, Day 5

Nothing Can Separate Us from God's Love...

This week's reflections have reminded us of God's lavish, compassionate, unfailing, and gentle love. We've seen that, even in the midst of suffering and pain, God loves us and desires to draw us closer to His heart. Today we will experience the truth that *nothing* can separate us from God's perfect love!

Please read each passage. Ask God to open the eyes of your heart so that you will understand what He is saying to you.

1. Rom: 8:31b: "If God is for us, who can be against us?"

   A. What does it mean to you that God is "for you"?

   B. Who or what attempts to come between you and God?

2. Rom. 8:35, 37–39: "Who shall separate us from the love of Christ? Shall trouble or hardship or persecution or famine or nakedness or danger or sword…? 37 No, in all these things we are more than conquerors through Him who loved us. 38 For I am convinced that neither death nor life, neither angels nor demons, neither the present nor the future, nor any powers, 39 neither height nor depth, nor anything else in all creation, will be able to separate us from the love of God that is in Christ Jesus our Lord."

   A. Verse 35 mentions "trouble" and "hardship." Why do troubles and hardships sometimes make us feel that the Lord has forgotten us and that we are separated from His love?

   B. Have you ever felt abandoned by the Lord, especially in regards to your child? Please write about your thoughts. *(This is a personal reflection question. You won't have to share this in your group.)*

   C. After reading this text, how would you answer Paul's question in verse 35, "Who shall separate us from the love of Christ?"

   D. Be creative and come up with a few other things that will *not* be able to separate you from the love of Christ! I'll get you started:

- neither unpaid bills nor a forgotten therapy appointment

- neither a raging child nor a critical in-law.

Now it's your turn:

- neither _____ nor _____

- neither _____ nor _____

- neither _____ nor _____

E. How are we, as God's people, described in verse 37?

F. According to this verse, who—and what—gives us the strength to be "more than conquerors"?

The definition of a conqueror is a "person who conquers or vanquishes; a victor. A conqueror defeats or subdues by force."[7] As Christians, our strength—our force—comes through Jesus Christ. Paul reminds us in Philippians 4:13 that "we can do all things through Christ, who gives us strength." When frustrations come and you're feeling overwhelmed, what an awesome prayer! *"I **can** handle all things through Christ. My strength comes from Him!"*

The New Living Translation of Romans 8:37 reads this way: "No, despite all these things, overwhelming victory is ours through Christ, who loved us." In Christ, we are the winner, the champion, the overwhelming *Victor*!

What wondrous love! *Nothing* will ever separate us from God's love. It covers us like silky skin. God is on our side and He deeply, passionately loves us. Psalm 91 says that all who "dwell in the shelter of the Most High will rest in the shadow of the Almighty." There is nothing that can overshadow God's shadow! When we dwell with Him, we can rest secure knowing that His love and power completely encompass us. And *nothing* can change that!

3. How did the Lord speak to you today?

---

7   *Dictionary.com Unabridged*, (Random House, Inc. 08 Mar. 2011), <Dictionary.com http://dictionary.reference. com/browse/conqueror>.

WALKING THE JOURNEY

There are times I have anger issues with God and I wonder why this happened to us. But then I read a devotional and realize that God will not give us more than we can handle. Also, there are times when we go to Maria's doctor's appointments and see other kids who are much worse off than she is. At times like that we are humbled and realize that we don't really have it that bad. We're thankful that Maria can walk and talk.

The fact that Maria is handicapped has also affected her sibling. Our older daughter, Taylor, feels that we love Maria more than we love her (which is not true, but it's how she feels), just because we do more things for Maria. They do behave like regular siblings though. They fight like normal kids, but yet when it comes down to it, they sincerely love each other and will do anything to protect one another. We've found out through the years that if we want Taylor to do something for her sister, we need to make it seem like her idea. For example, when Maria was starting kindergarten, we told Taylor that she may need to help her sister get on the bus. Taylor's response was, "Ugh, I always have to help my sister." But then the next day Taylor came up to me and said, "Hey, Mom, do you know what? When Maria and I go to school I can walk her to her classroom because I walk right past her room to go to mine."

Friends and family members are also sensitive to Maria's needs but it gets a little frustrating because we are not the type of people to want others to feel sorry for us. My mother-in-law tells her friends about Maria's difficulties and makes it look worse than it really is. Then they come up to us and say how sad it is that Maria is going through all this. However, we just tell them that she's a real trooper, and that she takes it all in stride.

Written by Sarah, whose young daughter, Maria, was born with physical handicaps and learning disabilities.

WEEK 2

Discovering Trust

"Trust in the Lord with all your heart and lean not on
your own understanding. In all your ways acknowledge
Him, and He will make your paths straight."

Prov. 3:5–6

Do you trust God? Not just trust *in* Him—but really trust *Him.* If you look in your Bible concordance you will find verse after verse about trust. In fact, most of us probably have a favorite Bible passage on trust. Mine is Proverbs 3:5–6: "Trust in the Lord with all your heart and lean not on your own understanding. In all your ways acknowledge Him, and He will make your paths straight." I can't tell you the times I've whispered that verse to myself when the twists in my life's journey have tied my stomach into knots.

What is it that keeps us from fully trusting God? Why is this so difficult? In fact, why *does* the Lord speak so often about trust? What holds us back from the childlike faith and trust that God desires from us?

This week we're going to study several passages in Scripture that focus on trust. We'll come to see how our fears, our unbelief, and our worries hold us back from jumping—without restraint—into His open arms. Along the way, we will discover both His patience with us and His perfect response to our lack of trust. We will uncover an amazing truth: when we believe that *God is who He says He is*, we will be able to relinquish our struggles, our troubles, our frustrations, and *ourselves* to Him with joyful abandon!

WEEK 2, DAY 1

WHY ME?

If there's any question I've asked God over and over, it would be this one: "Why me?" In some of my more angry and crabby moments, I've whined and complained to God about this child He chose to bless us with. But I've also genuinely asked this question in moments of raw honesty and searching. More than once, I've sincerely questioned God, asking, "What made You think I was capable of parenting such a difficult child?"

Do you ever wonder if God made a mistake in choosing *you* to be the mom of a child with such incredible needs? I can't see into your home, but I can guess you have days when you're angry, impatient, unloving, resentful, and full of doubts. Surely God could have (and should have?!) chosen a better home for your child.

Let's see what God's Word says about this.

Please read this passage. Ask God to open the eyes of your heart so that you will understand what He is saying to you.

1. Acts 17:24–28a: "The God who made the world and everything in it is the Lord of heaven and earth and does not live in temples built by hands. 25 And He is not served by human hands, as if He needed anything, because He Himself gives all men life and breath and everything else. 26 From one man He made every nation of men, that they should inhabit the whole earth; and He determined the times set for them and the exact places where they should live. 27 God did this so that men would seek Him and perhaps reach out for Him and find Him, though He is not far from each one of us. 28 'For in Him we live and move and have our being.'"

   A. List five truths these verses tell us about God (There are several!)

      1.

      2.

      3.

      4.

      5.

   B. Acts 17:25 tells us that "[God] is not served by human hands." What do you think this means? What answer does this verse reveal?

C. Who created your child? Who gave your child life and breath?

D. We're told in Acts 17:25 that God gives all people life, breath, and *everything else*. What are some things besides "life and breath" that God has given your child (i.e. any special talents, attributes, gifts, etc.)?

E. What are some things beside "life and breath" that God has given you? More specifically, with what has God gifted you?

F. Read Acts 17:26 several times. Let the meaning of these beautiful words wash over you. Spend a few minutes meditating on them and then answer these questions:

1. Who determined that your child would be your child? Was it a *coincidence* that your child was given to you?

2. What else is God saying to you in this verse? What is He whispering to your heart?

G. In essence, Acts 17:27 answers one of our "why" questions. *"Why did God determine that my child would be born at this time, with these needs, and placed in my home (either by birth or adoption)?"*

1. Find the answer to this question by reading Acts 17:27 from the first-person point of view and fill in the blanks. "God did this so that I would _____ _____ and perhaps _____ _____ for Him and _____ Him, though He is not far from me."

2. Do you tend to view God as a gracious, personal, loving God or as an impersonal, indifferent, hands-off God? (*This is a personal reflection question. You will not need to share this in your group.*)

3. God desires for us to seek Him and to reach out for Him. In doing so, He promises we *will* find Him, for He is not far from us. What do you think it means to "reach out" for God? How can we do this?

Bible commentaries define this "reaching out" as groping. When we're trying to find something in the dark, we claw around with uncertainty. But we worship Emmanuel, God with us! Because of this, we don't need to grope around with confusion or anxiety, not knowing if we'll ever really find God. God invites us to seek Him and reach out for Him with *confidence*, and He promises we will find Him. God is—by His very name and nature—a personal, "with us" God.

H. In light of all this exploration, how would you answer the question posed in the first paragraph: "Why me?" Why do *you* think God chose you to be the mom of a special-needs child?

2. What does any of this have to do with trust?

3. How did the Lord speak to you today?

WALKING THE JOURNEY

I feel as though God repeatedly gives us "something extra" with our kids, and I don't want it. I didn't want our son's disorder, but I'm stuck with it.

Do I think I can live with his disorder? Yes, I think I can. The problem lies in the fact that *I do not want to do it*. I feel as though so very, very little of my life is in my control And I know in my head that it isn't, but let me explain….

Maybe it's a jealousy thing. I see other people planning their lives and having their kids when they choose and their kids come out all fine and dandy. They are off to kindergarten in proper time without IEPs and one-on-one aides and diapers. No, I don't know their stories intimately, but it sure *seems* like there's an uneven balance there…(I'm thinking out loud, really.)

Okay, the more I write this, the more I realize this has a *lot* to do with my son's special needs. He's going through a horrific stage of hitting, scratching, pinching, and pulling hair, so much so that my four-year-old doesn't like to be near him. I am hyper-parenting him at all times. I cannot relax and enjoy life like I want to…I just…can't.

Yes, I do have an appointment with my therapist for next week, so don't worry too much, LOL. I just needed to get it out. I've already made some revelations in my head while writing this. Thanks for being part of our journey.

Tena's young son, Caden, was born with a rare disorder that causes mental retardation. This is an entry from her blog, http://thisisournormal.blogspot.com Used with permission.

WEEK 2, DAY 2

FEAR NOT!

Have you ever found yourself in the tight-fisted grip of *fear*? A fear so real that you have difficulty breathing, functioning, moving? Perhaps you experienced this kind of paralyzing fear when you first received your child's diagnosis. Maybe this fear wraps its tentacles around your heart when you look ahead to the future. Or just maybe you're living with this kind of fear right now. In yesterday's readings, we heard that God is a very loving and personal God who desires that we reach out for Him. What promises does God have for us when we find ourselves trapped in a deep pit of fear? Let's see what His precious Word tells us.

Please read each passage. Ask God to open the eyes of your heart so that you will understand what He is saying to you.

1. Is. 43:1–3a: "But now, this is what the LORD says—

   He who created you, O Jacob, He who formed you, O Israel:

   'Fear not, for I have redeemed you;

   I have summoned you by name; you are mine.

   2 When you pass through the waters,

   I will be with you;

   and when you pass through the rivers,

   they will not sweep over you.

   When you walk through the fire,

   you will not be burned;

   the flames will not set you ablaze.

   3 For I am the LORD, your God,

   the Holy One of Israel, your Savior.'"

   A. In these verses who is speaking? Who is listening?

The name Jacob means "follower; one who follows at the heel; deceiver." God changed Jacob's name to Israel after he spent an intense night wrestling with God (See Genesis 32:22–28.). The name Israel reflects this history: "he struggles with God." Listen to what God told Jacob when

He gave him his new name: "Your name will no longer be Jacob, but Israel, because you have struggled with God and with men and have overcome" (Gen. 32:28).

B. Now put *your* name in the place of Jacob and Israel. "...this is what the LORD says— He who created you, O _____, He who formed you, O _____: 'Fear not, for I have redeemed you; I have summoned you *by name*; you are mine.'"

C. Describe your struggle with God over your child's handicaps and challenges.

D. In Isaiah 43:1, what words and phrases appear that reveal the very personal and loving nature of God?

Redeem means to buy back; repurchase; to rescue (often from sin) with a ransom; to restore; to recover a possession.[8]

E. In Isaiah 43:1, we're told to "fear not." But the nature of the command implies that we are prone to struggle with fear. What do you most fear, especially for your child, your family, and yourself?

F. Carefully read Isaiah 43:2. What speaks to you in this verse? About what things, both positive and negative, can we be certain?

G. Now take these verses and make them personal to you. Put your name in the first blank. In the other blanks, fill in the fears that you listed above. Then bask in God's precious promises!

"_____, fear not! I've created you, I've formed you, and I've redeemed you. I know you and call you by your very own name; you are MINE! When _____, I will be with you; and even when _____, you won't drown. When _____, you won't be burned. Because I am the LORD your God, the Holy One of Israel, your Savior."

2. Is. 41:9b–10, 13: "...'You are my servant;

I have chosen you and have not rejected you.

10 So do not fear, for I am with you;

do not be dismayed, for I am your God.

I will strengthen you and help you;

I will uphold you with my righteous right hand....

13 For I am the LORD, your God

who takes hold of your right hand

and says to you, 'Do not fear;

I will help you.'"

---

8 The *Life Application Study Bible*, New International Version edition, Bible Dictionary, Notes and Bible Helps, (Tyndale House Publishers, 1988, 1989, 1990, 1991).

    A. How would you define the word *dismay* that appears in Isaiah 41:10?

    B. Why do you suppose the words *fear* and *dismay* appear together in this verse?

Dismay is defined as a disappointed feeling; distress. The thesaurus lists some synonyms of dismay as agitation, apprehension, discouragement, panic, and trepidation.[9]

    C. Think through the past twenty-four hours. Name a few events that led you to feel dismayed.

    D. According to these verses, what (Who!) is the antidote for our fear and dismay? How does the Lord promise to help us?

    E. What do these three passages on fear have to do with *trust?*

Beth Moore, author, writes, "The most critical breakthrough of faith you and I could ever experience is to let God bring us to a place where we trust Him—period. We don't just trust Him to let us avoid what we fear most. We determine to trust Him no matter what, even if our worst nightmare befalls us. We have no greater victory and can render Satan no harsher blow."[10]

3. How did the Lord speak to you today?

---

9   *Roget's 21st Century Thesaurus, Third Edition*, (Philip Lief Group 2009. 08 Mar. 2011). <Thesaurus.com http://thesaurus.com/browse/dismay>.

10 Beth Moore, *Esther, It's Tough Being a Woman*; workbook (LifeWay Press, 2008) 107, 108.

WALKING THE JOURNEY

My husband and I adopted three sisters from his cousin to add to our family of four biological children. The twins were adopted at ten weeks, and their older sister was five and one-half years old. As a family, we all thought this was a wonderful thing to keep the girls in the same family. Taylor, who was five and one-half, knew us and spent time with us—and most of all she loved us—so we hoped for an easy transition.

Circumstances played a toll on her though, and it was too much for a child of that age to work through. We tried counseling, we tried attachment therapy, we tried "date nights" with just Taylor, we tried talking, and most of all, we continued loving her—but nothing worked. It has been six years, and a roller coaster of emotions. It has taken a toll on her, on our family, and on me as a mother. Lying, stealing, deliberate disobedience, hoarding and gorging of food and things, no friends, immaturity, cutting, destruction of property—all these things are daily issues that hurt our other children, our marriage, and me as I watch her do these things.

I find myself angry and bitter at God at times for not hearing my prayers and for letting me feel alone with this journey. Yet, I find myself unable to give up hope that we will finally tear down the walls that she has built around her heart, and eventually see her become a whole person, a happy person, and a person who feels the love that I try to give. It is like a teeter-totter; some days I allow myself to be sad about it, and on other days I am on a crusade to better myself, my parenting, and my relationship with my daughter. But every day I am sad that I have so little a support system, because it is easier for family to ignore what they don't see.

As I experience all these emotions, I hold on to one verse, and repeat it to myself on good days and on bad days…the verse is 2 Thessalonians 3:13: "Never tire of doing what is right". Whatever the outcome will be, whatever the ending of our story, I pray for a happy ending. I believe that God is with me wherever we are on our walk with Reactive Attachment Disorder.

Lisa's young daughter, Taylor, has Reactive Attachment Disorder.

Week 2, Day 3

I Believe—Help My Unbelief!

Yesterday we looked at how fear affects us. I'm sure you could think of countless forces that bring you fear and dismay. We discovered that God has *promised* to be with us in every trial we face. He reaches out, takes our hand, and walks through our days with us. We can find assurance that even in our greatest difficulties and heartaches, God is still *God*. He's aware of our pain and fear, and we can trust Him to hold us close as we go through the floods and fires of life.

Did you know that the command "fear not" or "do not be afraid" is the most common command in Scripture? God knows how we are made. He knows that we are not born with an immense amount of courage! Today we're going to look at faith and belief, and see how it affects our trust in God. We're also going to learn how our faith can be *increased*. When we offer God even the smallest amount of genuine faith, He loves to increase it beyond our wildest imagination!

Please read each passage. Ask God to open the eyes of your heart so that you will understand what He is saying to you.

1. Mark 5:36: "Ignoring what they said, Jesus told [Jairus] the synagogue ruler, 'Don't be afraid; just believe.'"

Jairus had come to Jesus, pleading with Him to come to his home and heal his little girl. His daughter was dying, and he believed that if Jesus would come and lay His hands on her, she would be healed and would live. Jesus agreed to go with him. As they went on their way, though, a large crowd pressed in upon Jesus. A woman who had suffered from bleeding for twelve years came up behind Jesus, touched the hem of his cloak, and experienced immediate healing. Jesus stopped and gently explained to the woman—and to the crowd—what had just happened. He told her that her faith had healed her, that she was freed from her suffering, and that she could now "go in peace."

While Jesus was talking to the woman, some men came to Jairus and gave him some heartbreaking news. His precious little girl had just died; so he had no need to bother Jesus anymore. (This is my paraphrase of Mark 5:22–35.).

In Mark 5:36 we overhear Jesus' response to Jairus. "Ignoring what they said, Jesus told [Jairus] the synagogue ruler, 'Don't be afraid; just believe.'"

A. Reread Mark 5:36. On whom is Jesus focusing His attention?

B. Who and what was He ignoring?

C. What two commands did Jesus give Jairus?

    1.

    2.

D. Does this seem too simplistic to you? Why or why not?

What does *unbelief* (or lack of faith) have to do with fear? Have you ever thought of them as totally opposing viewpoints? I've heard it said that fear is the archenemy of faith. So, how do we develop a "fear not, only believe" kind of faith? Let's see what God's Word says....

2. Rom. 10:17: "Consequently, faith comes from hearing the message, and the message is heard through the word of Christ."

This is the same passage in the NLT: "So faith comes from hearing, that is, hearing the Good News about Christ."

The Amplified Bible presents the verse like this: "So faith comes by hearing [what is told], and what is heard comes by the preaching [of the message that came from the lips] of Christ [the Messiah Himself]."

A. How would you define "faith"?

B. What is one way we develop faith, according to Romans 10:17?

My Bible dictionary defines faith as "reliance, loyalty, or complete trust in God."[11] *Faith* is total dependence on God and a willingness to do His will.

C. What is the message of Good News we are to hear?

D. What are some practical ways you can *hear* the Good News? List as many as come to mind. (Don't limit yourself only to hearing with your ears!)

3. Gal. 5: 22, 23: "But the fruit of the Spirit is love, joy, peace, patience, kindness, goodness, faithfulness, gentleness and self-control."

Jesus said to His disciples in John 14:26, "But the Counselor, the Holy Spirit, whom the Father will send in my name, will teach you all things and will remind you of everything I have said to you."

---

11 The *Life Application Study Bible,* New International Version edition, Bible Dictionary, Notes and Bible Helps, (Tyndale House Publishers, 1988, 1989, 1990, 1991).

    A. Fill in the blank. In the Galatians passage, "faithfulness" is evidence or "fruit" of the
_____ living in us.

    B. According to John 14:26, what does Jesus tell us the Holy Spirit will do?

    C. How does having the Spirit living in us help us develop faith?

In Galatians 5:22–23, "faithfulness" is revealed to be a characteristic of the Holy Spirit. When we join our lives to Jesus Christ and experience the Holy Spirit living in us, His power enables us to develop His traits. Faith comes with the Holy Spirit!

John 14:26 ties together with Romans 10:17. The Holy Spirit, our Counselor, reminds us of the Good News Jesus taught when He lived on earth. In order to know this Good News, we need to read and to study His Word.

4. In Mark 9:24, a distraught father is pleading with Jesus to heal his demon-possessed son: "I do believe; help me overcome my unbelief!" In Luke 17:5, "The apostles said to the Lord, 'Increase our faith!'"

    A. According to these verses, what is another way our faith can be increased?

    B. Where does your faith seem to be the weakest, especially with respect to your child? (*This is a personal reflection question. You will not need to share this in your group.*)

    Stop for a minute and sincerely ask God to increase your faith.

5. The apostle writes in Ephesians 3:12: "Because of Christ and our faith in Him, we can now come boldly and confidently into God's presence" (NLT). Later, in Ephesians 3:20, he adds, "Now to Him who is able to do immeasurably more than all we ask or imagine, according to His great power within us…."

    A. What enables us to approach God with boldness and confidence?

    B. What would you most like to ask God, if you could talk to Him face to face?

Now picture yourself in the throne room of God and see Him gently reaching out to you. Go ahead, sit at His feet, and tell Him what's on your heart. Ask Him your deepest questions, and tell Him your heart's desire.

    C. What beautiful promise does Ephesians 3:20 contain?

Today we've seen that faith comes from hearing the Word of God and discovered that faith is a characteristic of the Holy Spirit—evidence that He lives in us. We can confidently ask God to help us overcome our lack of faith and boldly implore Him to increase our faith. How incredible it is to know that God is able to do *immeasurably more* than we ask or imagine!

As moms of special needs kids, we struggle with all sorts of challenges and heartaches—ones that demand much faith. But if our faith were never challenged, it would remain unchanged. Let's go before God's throne, release our fears, and ask our Heavenly Father to increase our faith. "Lord, I believe; help me overcome my unbelief!"

6. How did the Lord speak to you today?

WALKING THE JOURNEY

I refuse to believe that the Lord won't bring Johnny out of this! Some people may call my attitude denial. I don't. The Lord is in the process of healing Johnny. He's improved a lot over the last three years. Sometimes I think that maybe God allowed this to happen to Johnny because he knows the kind of man my husband is—a true warrior and pit bull at heart. When Johnny gets well, I truly believe my husband is going to devote the rest of his life to exposing Big Pharmaceutical*.

It would be too much for me to take if I didn't truly believe the Lord is in the process of healing our Johnny. I surely have been frustrated with the process that seems awfully slow to me. I know I'm to be thankful for the process, and now and then I actually am! But there surely is a lot of suspense in the meantime.

Jana's son, Johnny, has been diagnosed with autism.

*Johnny had been healthy and bright before having his eighteen-month shots.

WEEK 2, DAY 4

TRUSTING IN HIS PRESENCE

In yesterday's chapter, we learned that we could ask the Lord to increase our faith. We received the reassurance that He has promised to do immeasurably more than we even ask or imagine! Today we're going to look at several Scripture passages that will remind us that God never truly leaves us alone (even though we often feel isolated in our struggles and pain). He is walking this journey with us.

Please read each passage. Ask God to open the eyes of your heart so that you will understand what He is saying to you.

1. Isa: 42:16: "I will lead the blind by ways they have not known,

   along unfamiliar paths I will guide them;

   I will turn the darkness into light before them

   and make the rough places smooth.

   These are the things I will do;

   I will not forsake them."

   A. The word 'blind' is defined as "unable to see; sightless; unwilling or unable to perceive or understand." In what ways have you felt "blind" as a mom to a child with special needs?

   B. What are some "unfamiliar paths" you've traveled on your journey?

   C. What are some of the "rough places" you've encountered along the way?

   I love the way the Contemporary English Version of Isaiah 42:16 reads:

   I will lead the blind on roads

   they have never known;

   I will guide them on paths

   they have never traveled.

   Their road is dark and rough,

   but I will give light to keep them from stumbling.

   This is my solemn promise.

    D. Underline or highlight all of the "solemn promises" God gives us in this verse.

    E. How have you seen and experienced God's presence with you on your journey? How has He guided you and given you light?

2. Mark 6:47–51: "When evening came, the boat was in the middle of the lake, and He was alone on land. 48 Jesus saw the disciples straining at the oars, because the wind was against them. About the fourth watch of the night He went out to them, walking on the lake. He was about to pass by them, 49 but when they saw Him walking on the lake, they thought He was a ghost. They cried out, 50 because they all saw Him and were terrified. Immediately He spoke to them and said, 'Take courage! It is I. Don't be afraid.' 51 Then He climbed into the boat with them, and the wind died down. They were completely amazed."

    A. Where were the disciples during the storm? Where was Jesus?

    B. Do you think the disciples saw Jesus when He was still on the land?

    C. What do you imagine was the disciples' focus?

    D. Did Jesus see the disciples?

    E. What did Jesus do? What did He say to them?

    F. What caused the disciples to calm down? What amazed them?

One of my favorite names for God is *El Roi* (EL raw-EE), which means "the God who sees me." Hagar, an Egyptian slave woman of Sarai, Abram's wife, gave this name to God. She had encountered God in the desert when she was fleeing from the mistreatment of Sarai. Then she addressed God as *El Roi.* (You can read the entire account in Genesis 16:1–16.)

We can take such comfort in knowing that Jesus always sees us. He is always present, even if we don't immediately realize it. Jesus knows that at times our faith is weak and our fears immense, but He's not about to let us sink into the sea of despair! He longs for us to focus on *Him,* and not on our fears. Sometimes we question Jesus' timing, especially when we're exhausted to the bone. That's when we can identify with Jesus' disciples in the Mark passage, where we see that Jesus waited until the "fourth watch of the night," probably about 3:00–6:00 a.m., to come out to them. But Jesus always makes His presence known at just the right time. He instructs us to "take courage," He climbs into the boat with us, and He carries our burdens. His very presence calms our fears and stills our anxieties. We can trust Him at all times. His Presence never leaves us. El Roi never slumbers, never sleeps.

Let's close today's lesson by reading and meditating on Psalm 121.

    1 I lift up my eyes to the hills—

    where does my help come from?

    2 My help comes from the LORD,

the Maker of heaven and earth.

3 He will not let your foot slip—

he who watches over you will not slumber;

4 indeed, he who watches over Israel

will neither slumber nor sleep.

5 The LORD watches over you—

the LORD is your shade at your right hand;

6 the sun will not harm you by day,

nor the moon by night.

7 The LORD will keep you from all harm—

he will watch over your life;

8 the LORD will watch over your coming and going

both now and forevermore.

When you're exhausted, scared, and at your wit's end, invite Jesus to come into the boat with you. Just close your eyes for a moment and see Him sitting there with you. Draw courage from His presence. Then hear the words that God spoke to Moses while he faced life in the desert, both real and spiritual: "My Presence will go with you and I will give you rest" (Ex. 33:14).

3. How did the Lord speak to you today?

WALKING THE JOURNEY

We just got back from a youth group parents' meeting, and—boy!—did we ever feel like fish out of water. What a stark reminder that the challenges we face with our son are so different from those of other parents. We divided into small groups and were told to share the "joys and challenges of our teenagers." While other parents talked about curfews and clothing, parties and peer pressure, we just sat there silently (hoping that no one would expect us to join in).

Our reality was that our son, because of his anxiety disorder, had a painful meltdown since one of us wouldn't stay home with him. When we got home he was outside in the dark, on his bike. He didn't dare stay in the house because he thought he heard a voice say his name. He was scared to death. Now there's a challenge. But not one we would choose to openly share with the other high school parents.

I know I shouldn't dwell on it. Tomorrow will be another day. But tonight I just feel really down. I haven't felt like this for a long time…. It's just that, once in awhile, reality rears its ugly head.

An entry from my personal journal when our son was entering high school.

ENGRAVED ON HIS HANDS

"My Presence will go with you and I will give you rest" (Ex. 33:14). What a beautiful promise! I hope you hear those words often from your heavenly Father. He loves you so much! Today we're going to come to a deeper understanding of how very much He values us. We're going to look closely at the hands of Jesus and see whose image is inscribed in those gentle palms.

Please read each passage. Ask God to open the eyes of your heart so that you will understand what He is saying to you.

1. Isa. 49:13–16a: "Shout for joy, O heavens;

   rejoice, O earth;

   burst into song, O mountains!

   For the LORD comforts his people

   and will have compassion on his afflicted ones.

   14 But Zion said, 'The LORD has forsaken me,

   the Lord has forgotten me.'

   15 Can a mother forget the baby at her breast

    and have no compassion on the child she has borne?

   Though she may forget, I will not forget you!

   16 See, I have engraved you on the palms of my hands."

   A. Underline or highlight the reasons for "shouting, rejoicing, and bursting into song" listed in verse 13.

   B. We learned in our introductory lesson that "feelings of compassion are usually accompanied by acts of compassion." To whom is God directing His comfort and compassion?

Who comes to your mind when you hear the phrase "afflicted ones"? If you're like me, you probably immediately think of your own child (as in the comment, "he's afflicted with a mental illness") or someone who is extremely ill and enduring much suffering. But for a moment, I'd like you to put *yourself* in that place. My Bible dictionary defines *affliction* as "great suffering that produces sorrow."[12]

C. What affliction are you currently facing? What causes you great sorrow?

D. Have you ever felt like Zion was described in verse 14? Have you ever felt totally forsaken, forgotten, and abandoned by the Lord? What made you feel like that? (*This is a personal reflection question. You will not need to share this in your group.*)

E. How does the Lord answer Zion's outcry in verses 15 and 16?

F. Is it even remotely possible for God to forget our children or us? On what do you base your answer?

To engrave literally means "to carve; cut." According to the thesaurus, one of the synonyms of engrave is *infix*. To infix means to "implant so deeply as to make change nearly impossible."[13] Listen to how the Amplified Bible translates Isaiah 49:16: "Behold, I have indelibly imprinted (tattooed a picture of) you on the palm of each of My hands…."

G. Whose name and image is engraved, carved into, indelibly printed (tattooed) on the Lord's palm? Write it in capital letters! (Go ahead…you have permission not only to write your name, but also the names of those you love more than anyone else in the world!)

Reflect for just a moment on the familiar words of Isaiah 53:5a, "He was pierced for our transgressions…." The hands of Jesus bear the mark of what He endured for us. He loves us so much that He willingly held out His hands and gave His life for us.

Jesus did not die for us to simply forget about us. He literally cut our names into His palms. Each time He reaches out to comfort you, He sees your name. Each time He glances at His palms, He sees the very image of your precious child. Can you trust Him with your life? Can you trust Him with your child's life?

2. Ps. 31:14–15: "But I trust in you, O LORD; I say, 'You are my God.' 15 My times are in your hands; deliver me from my enemies and from those who pursue me."

Here is the same passage in the NLT: "But I am trusting you, O Lord, saying, 'You are my God!' 15 My future is in your hands. Rescue me from those who hunt me down relentlessly."

Another version presents the passage like this: "Desperate, I throw myself on you: you are my God! 15 Hour by hour I place my days in your hand, safe from the hands out to get me" (MSG).

---

12 The *Life Application Study Bible,* New International Version edition, Bible Dictionary, Notes and Bible Helps, (Tyndale House Publishers, 1988, 1989, 1990, 1991).

13 *Roget's 21st Century Thesaurus, Third Edition,* (Philip Lief Group 2009. 08 Mar. 2011), <Thesaurus.com http://thesaurus.com/browse/engrave>.

A. In whom was the Psalmist placing his trust?

B. How did he know that he could trust the Lord?

C. Read all three versions of verse 15. Fill in the blanks.

    1. NIV: My _____ are in your hands.

    2. NLT: My _____ is in your hands.

    3. The Message: _____ by _____ I place my _____ in your hands.

D. *What* is safe and secure in God's hands?

E. Carefully read the second part of verse 15. From what or from whom is the Psalmist asking for deliverance?

F. When you consider your life as a mom to a child with special needs, what—but not necessarily who—do you consider to be your enemy? What seems to be pursuing you, hunting you down?

Do you worry about your child's future? Do you worry about *your* future? What causes you to lose sleep? Do you worry about finances, your marriage, your child's behaviors, or your child's educational issues (those dreaded IEPs!)? Do you anguish over who would take care of your child if you or your husband were to die? These are enemies that pursue us and seek to destroy us.

Satan is enemy number one. He comes only to "steal, kill, and destroy" (John 10:10a). He "prowls around like a roaring lion looking for someone to devour" (I Peter 5:8b). What should we do when we feel the hands of the enemy grabbing for us? When our minds are racing a hundred miles an hour in fear and anxiety? The Psalmist instructs us to throw ourselves upon God, placing our trust in Him. We need to do this day by day, hour by hour. Satan comes to destroy our families and us, but Christ came to bring us life—abundant life—in the fullest sense of the word!

Take to heart the very Words of God…meditate on them…memorize them. Tuck them deep in your heart so that when the enemy closes in, you can repeat in the ear of your heart God's promises to you. He will *never* let you fall. *You can trust Him.*

Take comfort in some words of consolation and encouragement from the Scriptures.

• "Cast your cares on the Lord and He will sustain you; He will never let the righteous fall" (Ps. 55:22).

• "Cast all your anxiety on Him because He cares for you" (1 Peter 5:7).

- "The Lord is good, a refuge in times of trouble. He cares for those who trust in Him" (Nah. 1:7).

- "You will keep in perfect peace him whose mind is steadfast, because he trusts in you. Trust in the Lord, the Lord, in the Rock eternal" (Isa. 26:3–4).

- "I will never leave you or forsake you" (Heb. 13:5).

3. How did the Lord speak to you today?

Walking the Journey

We have to admit that it has been difficult lately as we've become more aware of Cayla's delays. Even though we have known there would be delays, it has still been frustrating. Fine motor skills, gross motor skills, and speech are three of the areas where we haven't seen a whole lot of progress lately. By Cayla's age, most kids are walking or at least crawling. She isn't very close to walking and hasn't made a whole lot of progress with crawling either. But last night, she did decide to scoot backwards for us. Three scoots right in a row! It was amazing and we enjoyed it so much.

We are realizing that we're going to cherish every little gain she makes. In our impatience, we are reminding ourselves to trust God's timing in *everything*. Our journey with Cayla is going to be unique and filled with highs and lows, but God is good and it's nice to know that He loves Cayla so much more than either of us do.

Leah's little daughter, Cayla, has Down syndrome. This was posted on her blog, http://littlegarland. blogspot.com. Used with permission.

I do worry about Maria's future. There are certain things that she cannot do on her own, and I'm not sure if she ever will be able to do them. I worry about her living on her own and what her future may hold for her. Yeah, that is a concern to us.

Sarah's young daughter was born with physical handicaps and learning disabilities.

WEEK 3

The God of Hope

"The Lord delights in those who fear Him, who put their hope in His unfailing love."—Ps. 147:11

Hope. What comes to mind when you think of the word "hope"? From time to time we all find ourselves *hoping* for various things...a bigger house, a full night's sleep (!), a promotion, another child, good weather for an upcoming outing, a successful diet, a victory for our favorite team, and so on. Hope always brings to mind what we long to possess, what we expect for the future.

When we embarked on motherhood, we had stars in our eyes and hope in our hearts! We just knew that our child would be an amazing specimen of humanity. He or she would be gorgeous, kind and compassionate, would perform as a star athlete, an incredible musician, and a scholar at the top of the class. Other parents would compare their child with ours and find theirs lacking!

And then real life entered the picture. Your child was born with *special needs.* Or perhaps the child you adopted came home with more emotional burdens than you ever imagined.

As moms of children with special needs, we've had to readjust our hopes for our children. This especially happens during those "milestone" years. For example, we watch from the outside and see our child's peers racing off to kindergarten. Their parents are full of expectations of an enriching, exciting school career...dreaming of friendships, sports, dances, and accomplishments. Our dreams may be a little less lofty. We are hoping our child will *eventually* be potty-trained.

Or perhaps your child is entering middle school—a scary time for all children and their parents. But for you it's even more difficult. Because of an attachment disorder, your child has a tendency to lie, steal, and cheat. She has very few friends because of her inability to read social cues. You worry that she may become sexually active. Your heart aches for her, and you're concerned about her future. You had such high hopes....

As Christians, we know that our hope must be in the *Lord.* But what, really, does that mean? My Bible dictionary defines "hope" this way: "To desire something with *confident expectation* of its fulfillment"[14] (italics added). How can this kind of hope transform our day-to-day lives? Just what *can* we confidently expect from the Lord in our everyday lives?

Let's go to the Word and see what the God of hope has to say....

---

14 The *Life Application Study Bible,* New International Version edition, Bible Dictionary, Notes and Bible Helps, (Tyndale House Publishers, 1988, 1989, 1990, 1991).

Week 3, Day 1

Show Me...Teach Me...Guide Me

Let's confidently ask the Lord to teach us about hope.

Please read each passage. Ask God to open the eyes of your heart so that you will understand what He is saying to you.

1. Ps. 25:4–5: "Show me Your ways, O LORD,

   teach me Your paths;

   5 guide me in Your truth and teach me,

   for You are God my Savior,

   and my hope is in You all day long."

   A. What is the Psalmist asking the Lord to do?

   B. Circle the words "me" and "my" each time they appear in these verses. Our God is such a personal God! Before we go any further, stop and pray these words to the Lord. Ask Him to show you, teach you, and guide you on your journey to a greater hope.

   C. Underline the words immediately following the word "Your" in these verses. Now list them here.

      1. Show me Your _____

      2. Teach me Your _____

      3. Guide me in Your _____

The words "way" and "path" make us think of a journey or a road we're traveling along. The ancient Hebrew people viewed life as a path. They were a nomadic people, wandering from place to place. They knew that if they left the path they would face dangers—wild animals and enemies. They realized that to stay on the path, they needed Someone to clearly show them the way. In this Psalm, David asked God for guidance. He fully trusted God to lead him.

In Psalm 25:4, David asked God to show him His *ways*. In verse 5 David asked God to guide him in *truth*. To get some additional insights, let's go to the New Testament and read from the book of John.

2. John 14:6: "Jesus said, 'I am the way, and the truth, and the life. No one comes to the Father except through me.'"

    A. Who is the embodiment of the way, the truth, and the life?

    B. What is the only way to the Father?

This verse tells us that Jesus is the *only* way to the Father—the *only* way to attain salvation. We will not get to heaven except by believing in and accepting the salvation that comes through the death and resurrection of Jesus. When we unite our life to Jesus, we are united with God. But how does that bring us hope here and now? We're not in heaven yet, so what hope does Jesus offer us for the struggles we face *today?* Please read and meditate on two powerful verses.

3. Paul writes in Romans 8:34, "Jesus Christ, who died—more than that, who was raised to life—is at the right hand of God and is also interceding for us." The apostle proclaims in Hebrews 7:25, "Therefore He is able to save completely those who come to God through Him, because He always lives to intercede for them."

    A. According to these verses, what is Jesus doing? (Notice the present tense of the question!)

    B. The "He" in the Hebrews passage refers to Jesus. Please fill in the blank. "Jesus always _____ to intercede for them." Consider some things *we* live for. We glibly say we *live for* the weekend...or we *live for* chocolate...or we *live for* our children. Imagine, Jesus tells us He *lives* so that He may intercede for us!

    C. What do you think it means to "intercede"?

One dictionary definition of intercede is to "act or interpose in behalf of someone in difficulty or trouble, as by pleading or petition; to mediate."[15] Some synonyms of the word "intercede" are advocate, intervene, plead, reconcile, and step in. Wow! That's what Jesus is doing for us!

On our dark days, when we feel as though we have no hope, we can go straight to the Father to renew our hope. Jesus, Himself, is the path—the way to our Father. Jesus stands before the Father *pleading* on our behalf. It is not only for our salvation that He intercedes, but also for everything that we sincerely bring before Him in prayer.

    D. What situation are you facing today that seems hopeless? (*This is a personal reflection question. You will not need to share this in your group.*)

---

15 *Dictionary.com Unabridged* (Random House, Inc. 08 Mar. 2011), <Dictionary.com http://dictionary.reference. com/browse/intercede>.

Please know that Jesus is praying for you. He sees your distress and He hears your cries for help. Right now Jesus is interceding for you and me. Because Jesus is interceding for us, we can be assured that God hears and answers our prayers. This doesn't mean that he will necessarily answer our prayers according to how *we* want Him to respond, but He will answer those prayers according to the will of our loving heavenly Father.

4. Ps. 6:8b–9: "For the Lord has heard my weeping. The Lord has heard my plea; the Lord will answer my prayer."

    A. What promises does the Lord give us in this passage?

    B. What hope, what confident expectation, does this give you for today's struggles and for your future?

5. How did the Lord speak to you today?

WALKING THE JOURNEY

Last Tuesday pretty much showed what my life has turned into so often these past six years, ever since Johnny got sick with what everybody calls autism. I had to keep him home from school to keep a required appointment with the local MHMR (Mental Health–Mental Retardation) office, for psychological testing. The first hour was an ordeal for Johnny, for me, and even for the staff at MHMR. Johnny often can't handle unfamiliar surroundings, and he couldn't handle this place either. He cried for the first hour until his face turned blotchy and he almost hyperventilated. He kept pulling my hand and taking me to the door. He just didn't understand why he had to be there, and I really didn't either. But the system requires it.

At the end of the evaluation, the social worker tried to tell me that Johnny is severely mentally retarded. I would not allow her to say the IQ number in Johnny's presence. He understands a lot, even though people think he's oblivious! If people only knew how incredibly bright Johnny had been before he got those eighteen-month shots! He was then doing lots of complex tasks that he could not begin to do now at age nine. He had been talking just as much as his fraternal twin brother, who somehow escaped the effects of the shots. However, within four days of those shots, we could tell that something had gone terribly wrong with Johnny. But none of the experts who now work with Johnny knew that other "before the shots" Johnny.

Jana's son, Johnny, has been diagnosed with autism.

A HOPE AND A FUTURE

Do you ever feel like you're living in captivity? I wouldn't even dare broach this subject in a typical Bible study! Most moms probably wouldn't understand the feelings that weigh upon my heart. But I trust you, so here I go. There are times when my husband and I say that we feel as though our son is holding us hostage! His demands, at times, are so great and the burden is so exhausting. When we look ahead, we don't see that it's going to change anytime soon. He probably won't be moving out of our home after high school. We're not sure what kind of job he'll be able to hold down. We likely will be supporting him (financially, emotionally, and in other ways) well into his adulthood. Mental illness doesn't go away as you get older. In fact, what if his gets worse? These are some of our thoughts and feelings as we look beyond today.

What about you? Do you ever feel as if you're living in bondage? Do you feel like the demands that your child and his or her condition place on you keep you in captivity? Are there times you wonder if you'll ever be able to pursue your dreams…your career…your future? Today, let's look at a familiar passage of Scripture and allow God's Word to break some chains!

Please read each passage. Ask God to open the eyes of your heart so that you will understand what He is saying to you.

1. Jer. 29:11–14a: "For I know the plans I have for you," declares the LORD, "plans to prosper you and not to harm you, plans to give you hope and a future. 12 Then you will call upon me and come and pray to me, and I will listen to you. 13 You will seek me and find me when you seek me with all your heart. 14 I will be found by you," declares the LORD, "and will bring you back from captivity."

   A. Underline the word "plans" in these verses. Who has the master plan for your life?

   B. According to verse 11, what kinds of plans does the Lord have for you? Please fill in the blanks. "Plans to _____ me and not to _____ me, plans to give me _____ and a _____."

   C. What do verses 12 and 13 tell us that God desires from us?

   D. According to verse 13, how does God tell us to seek Him?

   E. What do you think it means to seek God with "all your heart"?

F. What incredible promises are given in these verses?

G. Now let's personalize this a little more. What were some of the plans you made for your life when you were younger? What were your dreams and hopes?

Did you put "having a child with difficult needs and challenges" on your list? No? Do you wonder if somehow God messed up when He gave you a child with special needs? Do you feel like you're just spinning your wheels, biding your time until you can pursue your *real* calling in life? Does it seem like you have placed your life's calling on hold while you're stuck in this unfamiliar territory?

Let's back up a few verses and read the first part of Jeremiah 29. You see, when the prophet Jeremiah told the children of Israel that God had great plans and a promising hope for their future, they were literally living in captivity. They had been forced away from their homes, their cities, and all that was familiar, and were enslaved for seventy years in a distant and pagan nation.

2. Jer. 29:4–7: "This is what the LORD Almighty, the God of Israel, says to all those I carried into exile from Jerusalem to Babylon: 5 'Build houses and settle down; plant gardens and eat what they produce. 6 Marry and have sons and daughters; find wives for your sons and give your daughters in marriage, so that they too may have sons and daughters. Increase in number there; do not decrease. 7 Also, seek the peace and prosperity of the city to which I have carried you into exile. Pray to the LORD for it, because if it prospers, you too will prosper.'"

   A. What instructions does the Lord give His people in these verses?

   B. In what ways have you been called into unfamiliar territory with your child?

   C. In these verses, the Lord instructs His children to go on with their lives, even during difficult times of trials. For many of us this "difficult time of trial" could expand across several years. What encouragement do we receive from these two passages? What will enable us to move ahead with confidence, instead of giving up in fear and uncertainty? (See especially verses 7, 12, and 13.)

   D. Re-read Jeremiah 29:11–14 (from question 1). What *hope* do you find in these verses? Look closely and list at least five.

      1.

      2.

      3.

      4.

      5.

Has God forgotten all about you and *your* dreams and desires for your life? Does your future seem bleak…and your present circumstances even bleaker? Dear sister, God's plans will most certainly prosper you. It's just that His plans often look different from our plans. But God really does know what He's doing! He has the power to take this difficult challenge and turn it into His calling for your life. I like what I once heard Dr. Adrian Rogers say: "Jesus had some scars; and if you follow Him, so will you. Your scars may be your greatest ministry."

If you feel as though you're living in captivity, please don't stop *living*. Keep Christ as your center, continue to seek Him, and step into each day with the hope and confidence that God can and will use you, even in—*especially in*—your present circumstances.

3. How did the Lord speak to you today?

Walking the Journey

The other day I was thinking about work issues, specifically about how having a bipolar child affects our lives—beyond the obvious day-to-day stressors. I had to give up going for a career I've dreamed of since I was a kid. I was studying to be a Lutheran pastor, but the committee felt I shouldn't continue with such "difficult" family members—even though I was a straight-A student (with these family members!). I love my job now, but I hang on day to day. My daughter and my husband call me all the time; not to mention the doctors, the school, etc. I am trying to manage their lives while trying to bring in an income.

Then, of course, there are the morning struggles. Should I be late for work again and get Zoe into school, or take truancy charges and get to work on time? I recently cut back to part-time because the issues, phone calls, and appointments were getting to be too much. Thus a cut in salary means more financial stress. Mental illness issues affect family life in so many ways.

Meg's teenage daughter, Zoe, has bipolar disorder.

FINDING HOPE IN THE BIGGER PICTURE

"And we know that in all things God works for the good of those who love Him, who have been called according to His purpose" (Rom. 8:28). People often quote this verse, intending to offer quick and helpful encouragement to others experiencing heartache, pain, suffering, and grief. Perhaps some well-meaning people shared this verse with you following the birth of your child (or at some other difficult time in your life). Did it comfort you or did it make you mad? Do you wonder what good could possibly come from having a child with such problems and needs?

Today we're going to look a little deeper into the promise that God has a bigger picture and purpose for our lives. We may not always see His intentions in the midst of the pain of our circumstances, but God has made a promise, so we can believe Him and trust Him to keep that promise.

Please read each passage. Ask God to open the eyes of your heart so that you will understand what He is saying to you.

1. Rom. 8:28–29: "And we know that in all things God works for the good of those who love Him, who have been called according to His purpose. 29 For those God foreknew He also predestined to be conformed to the likeness of His Son, that He might be the firstborn among many brothers."

   The same passage appears in another translation: "And we know that God causes everything to work together for the good of those who love God and are called according to His purpose for them. 29 For God knew His people in advance, and He chose them to become like His Son, so that His Son would be the firstborn among many brothers and sisters" (Rom. 8:28–29, NLT)

   A. According to Romans 8:28, for whose good is God working?

   B. Fill in the blanks to discover afresh just how complete God's promise is in this verse. "And we know that _____ _____ _____ God works for the good of those who love Him…." According to the New Living Translation, "And we know that God causes _____ to work together for the good of those who love God…."

   C. According to this verse, is there anything outside of God's ability to work for our good?

D. In your life, where do you have a hard time believing this? (*This is a personal reflection question. You will not need to share this in your group.*)

E. In Romans 8:28, Paul reminds us, "God works in all things for our _____."

We cannot say that everything that happens *to* us is good. We know that is not true. We live in a broken and sinful world. But we know that God is able to turn every circumstance around for our ultimate good. Note also that we cannot say that God works to make us *happy* (although this often is a blessed occurrence!). Instead, we must look closely at Romans 8:29 to see what this "good" looks like.

F. Reread Romans 8:29 in both versions. Whom did God choose us to become like?

We really can't separate verses 28 and 29. God's ultimate plan and purpose for our lives are to make us more and more like Jesus! Whatever suffering God allows to come into our lives He uses to conform us to the image of His precious Son. Simply put, God wants us to look like Jesus! What does Jesus look like? What trials and difficult circumstances (besides His crucifixion), did He have to endure? Let's take a look at a few ways that Jesus suffered.

- People rejected Him, even though He loved and cared for everyone. *Jesus understands when we experience rejection from the people closest to us.*

- Jesus had to deal with being misunderstood, even by His most devoted disciples. *Jesus knows what we're going through when we feel misunderstood and judged by other parents, family members, school teachers, and church members.*

- Jesus suffered physically and emotionally through hunger and temptation. *Jesus doesn't condemn us when we're tempted to overeat or drink to fill the ache. Instead, He provides a better way. He says "Come to me when you're burdened and weighed down with grief.... I'll carry the load. You just rest."*

- Jesus experienced times of intense discouragement, sadness, and grief. *He mourns with my husband and me over our son's mental illness and with you over your child's struggles. He understands how this discourages us and makes us sad.*

- Jesus loved the whole world and even died for everyone (see John 3:16), but so many reject His love and do not love Him in return. Even His children too often take His love for granted and forget what it cost Him. *Jesus knows exactly how it feels when our kids don't reciprocate our love...or say they hate us.*

Yes, Jesus suffered much, but through it all He remained perfect and untainted by sin. Let's look at some of His attributes to better understand Jesus and His suffering.

2. Ps. 103:8–14, (NLT) The Lord is compassionate and merciful, slow to get angry and filled with unfailing love. 9 He will not constantly accuse us, nor remain angry forever. 10 He does not punish us for all our sins; He does not deal harshly with us, as we deserve. 11 For His unfailing love toward those who fear Him is as great as the height of the heavens above the

earth. 12 He has removed our sins as far from us as the east is from the west. 13 The Lord is like a father to His children, tender and compassionate to those who fear Him. 14 For He knows how weak we are; He remembers we are only dust".

A. List at least ten attributes of the Lord that appear in these verses.

    1.

    2.

    3.

    4.

    5.

    6.

    7.

    8.

    9.

    10.

When you read the Gospels, you see example after example of Christ's compassion, love, gentleness, patience, faith, obedience, hope, encouragement, kindness, and so forth. He had an especially tender heart towards the people often considered the "least."

B. In what ways can you see that God has used your sufferings (especially over your child) to make you more Christ-like? Are you more patient? Are you more compassionate towards others with special needs? Are you more tolerant, kind, and loving? Please don't be shy! It's good to take note of how God has worked in your life, specifically *because* He has entrusted you with a child with special needs.

C. What steps can we take to get to know Christ better, so that He can increasingly conform us to His likeness?

3. How did the Lord speak to you today?

WALKING THE JOURNEY

It was Mother's Day. We went to Target, where I planned to return three items and come right back out. My hubby suggested we all go in together. He knows shopping is my favorite gig ever and bumming around Target for clearance is quite high up there on my fun list. Plus it *was* Mother's Day, but I should have known better. We piled all the kids into the store, and within a minute Caden, started his whining and grunting "I'm irritated" noise—mostly due to the fact that we don't allow him to take his pacifier into buildings. And he's loud. And of course people stared (this truly does *not bother* me, but I want you to be aware of what we're dealing with here). So we were trying to look for things here and there, and during this time Caden wandered off twice—instant "into the cart" rule. And he wasn't happy, so the whining began to crescendo. Long story short, we bought batteries and toilet paper, Daddy grabbed Caden and brought him to the van while I checked out with the other two (always the super troopers), and we headed home.

The ride home was pretty much silent. Caden fell asleep immediately. The silence was broken when I said to my husband, "Does it ever feel to you like Caden ruins most of our family outings?" While I don't wish (anymore) for Caden not to have his disorder, the truth is I wish very much for him to be more normal. I can't *fathom* what he would be like without his disorder, as it's the very essence of who he is, but I suppose I wish I could tailor his disorder to suit our family's needs better. And can you even imagine, do you even *know*, how much it breaks a mother's heart to wish that your kid wasn't the way he was? When I look at him, my hearts adores him, but in the very same heartbeat, I want something different for him, for all of us. I want it to be *fun* to go out and do things together as a family. I wish we didn't have to curb the things we do because Caden can't handle it, won't understand it, won't cooperate, doesn't understand consequences, so there's no punishment that works…. The list goes on.

And these are the moments you feel very, very alone. My husband doesn't get it in the same way I do. He doesn't deal with it as many hours as I do. I don't like asking for help. I feel like Caden's "my problem"—one I never asked for, but apparently I needed. And he acts so good for others! At home it's where we have the issues. I suppose that makes sense in terms of how we all behave differently at home, and I am glad he's obviously comfortable here. It's just…different.

I'm throwing this all out there for heaven-knows-what reason. Maybe because I think I inadvertently portray that everything's a-okay for us when it comes to Caden—and mostly, it is; but there are days that spiral downward so fast because it's all been building up. Maybe because these feelings are real and raw, and I think it needs to be okay to share them. And maybe because I just need a hug.

Tena's young son, Caden, has a rare disorder that causes mental retardation. This is an entry from her blog, http://www.thisisournormal.blogspot.com. Used with permission.

Week 3, Day 4

Joyful in Hope

Do you realize that we please God when we put our hope in Him? It's easy to become very self-focused in our day-to-day struggles with our kids. But as we discovered yesterday, we're part of a much bigger picture. Today we're going to look at how our hope delights the Lord.

Please read each passage. Ask God to open the eyes of your heart so that you will understand what He is saying to you.

1. Ps. 147:11: "The LORD delights in those who fear Him, who put their hope in His unfailing love."

   A. Fill in the blanks to discover in whom the Lord delights. "The Lord delights in those who _____ Him, who _____ _____ _____ in His unfailing love."

   B. Read the same verse in the Amplified version: "The Lord takes pleasure in those who reverently and worshipfully fear Him, in those who hope in His mercy and loving-kindness."

      In what, specifically, does God desire us to place our hope? Fill in the blanks using the words from both versions:

      1. His _____ _____ (NIV)

      2. His _____ and _____ _____ (Amplified Bible)

   C. Why do you think it delights the Lord when we put our fear (our reverence and awe) and our hope in Him?

   God desires our worship, our praise, our adoration…our hope. It gives Him great joy when we genuinely worship and trust Him!

2. Consider what Paul writes: "Be joyful in hope, patient in affliction, faithful in prayer" (Rom. 12:12). Another version presents the verse this way: "Rejoice in our confident hope. Be patient in trouble, and keep on praying" (Rom. 12:12, NLT)

   A. What are we to be joyful in?

B. As a believer, what gives you confident hope?

C. How are we to handle afflictions and troubles?

3. Ps. 33:18, 20–22: "But the eyes of the LORD are on those who fear Him, on those whose hope is in His unfailing love.... 20 We wait in hope for the LORD; He is our help and our shield. 21 In Him our hearts rejoice, for we trust in His holy name. 22 May Your unfailing love rest upon us, O LORD, even as we put our hope in You."

A. Who is the Lord watching over?

Do you get the sense that the Lord is keeping an especially close eye on His precious children? He loves all of His creation, but He takes special pleasure and delight in those who join Jesus in calling Him Abba, Father. When you bring your child to the park, you see all the children playing. You enjoy watching them laughing, running, swinging, sliding, and playing with abandon. However, don't you find your gaze going to *your* child more than to the others? Don't you take extra-special delight in *your* child's antics? Don't you grin and laugh when he's goofing off and just enjoying life? And aren't you the first one to jump up and run to him when he's hurt? You're the one who cuddles and holds him when he's crying in pain. You're the one who gently pulls the splinter out of his finger, who kisses and bandages his banged-up, bloody knees, and who wipes his tears away.

How would you feel if your child ran to another mother for comfort? If he pushed you away and told you that you caused his pain? No, you long for and expect your child to run to you when he's hurt. In the same way, the Lord longs for us to run to *Him* when we're hurting. He wants to be the One who holds us close, who comforts us, who bandages our wounds, and who wipes our tears away. The Lord *delights* in those who run to Him for help, who find their hope and comfort in Him.

B. How does the Psalmist describe the Lord in Psalm 33:20?

C. How does it give you hope to know that God is your help and shield?

D. When we put our hope—our confident expectation—in the Lord, what does the Psalm say will "rest upon us"?

4. Consider a few additional passages that tell us about the comfort God gives to us. "Find rest, O my soul, in God alone; my hope comes from Him" (Ps. 62:5) "Blessed is he whose help is the God of Jacob, whose hope is in the LORD his God" (Ps. 146:5). "The LORD is good to those whose hope is in Him, to the one who seeks Him" (Lam. 3:25).

A. List the promises given in these verses:

1. In Ps. 62:5, God promises _____ for those who put their hope in the Lord.

2. In Ps. 146:5, God tells us that those who put their hope in Him are _____.

3. In Lam. 3:25, we're told that the Lord is _____ to all who seek Him and put their hope in Him.

B. Close your eyes and envision the Lord opening His arms to you as you purposefully run to Him and entrust Him with your child, your life, and your troubles. Allow the Lord to comfort you with His love and give you rest as you put your hope in Him. He is delighted that you ran to Him…that you desired Him above all others. He has His arms wrapped tightly around you, soothing you, singing gently in your ear. Never forget that He delights in all who fear Him and put their hope in Him!

5. How did the Lord speak to you today?

WALKING THE JOURNEY

We honestly felt like we had finished our grieving a while ago. Being in social work, I have learned a lot about grieving and truly believed that we had crossed that bridge. However, as Cayla has grown older, we have come to understand that the process will continue for us.

One thing that has surprised us is the jealousy that can creep in now and again. Although we know Cayla will do everything in her own timing, it's sometimes hard to see her peers developing so much more quickly than she is. Not only is she behind in fine and gross motor skills, but she also has a flat affect.

It can be difficult to see people meet her and try to make her smile or laugh. Usually, she just stares at them or reaches for their face. Often, they don't know whether to try harder or give up. Even people she knows well have to work really hard to get a smile from her. We find ourselves making excuses sometimes, explaining that she's probably tired.

We've gone weeks without getting a giggle from her, and it can get frustrating. But when she does laugh, it is one of the best feelings in the world! She has a pretty smile and adorable laugh, but not many people have gotten to hear it. One thing, though—when she is giggling, you do anything you can to keep that puppy going! I recently made a fool of myself at Wal-Mart because Cayla was laughing, and I wanted to milk it for all it was worth!

Leah's little girl, Cayla, has Down syndrome. This was posted on her blog, http://littlegarland.blogspot. com. Used with permission.

Week 3, Day 5

Hope and Peace

Did you know that *hope* and *peace* often go together in the Bible? Why do you suppose that is? Today we'll look at a few passages where these two words appear together. Let's see what encouragement we can receive from God's precious Word.

Please read each passage. Ask God to open the eyes of your heart so that you will understand what He is saying to you.

1. Rom. 15:13: "May the God of hope fill you with all joy and peace as you trust in him, so that you may overflow with hope by the power of the Holy Spirit."

   A. How is God described in this verse?

   B. With what is the apostle Paul asking God to fill believers?

   C. What is necessary to receive this joy and peace?

   D. Why do you think trust is essential for joy, peace, and hope?

   E. Fill in the blanks to complete the verse: "May the God of hope _____ you with all joy and peace as you trust in Him, so that you may _____ with hope by the power of the Holy Spirit."

Now read this same verse in the Amplified Bible, "May the God of your hope so fill you with all joy and peace in believing [through the experience of your faith] that by the power of the Holy Spirit you may abound and be overflowing (bubbling over) with hope."

Have you ever been distracted when you were pouring a glass of milk or juice for your child? Before you knew it, the liquid was running down the sides of the glass, onto the table, and pooling on the floor. It was abundantly more than your child asked for! This is the word picture Paul uses to show how God longs to pour His hope into us. He wants to fill us with so much joy and peace that we're *abounding, overflowing, and bubbling over* with hope! This kind of hope, joy, and peace will come only by trusting the Lord with all in our lives—with fully surrendering to Him our cares, our worries, our anger, and our unbelief. We can open our arms with abandon and release to Him all that holds us back from experiencing the peace and joy He longs to give us. When we give up the junk in our lives, He fills us with His sweet peace and joy! And through the power of the Holy Spirit we abound and bubble over with *hope*!

    F. What "junk" do you need to get rid of in order to make space in your heart for God's hope and peace? (In my life I struggle with a fear for my son's future. I have no idea what it will look like. Over and over again, I need to release my fears and worries to God, and ask Him to fill me with His peace). Do you have any particular thing you struggle with? What's your junk?

2. Rom. 5: 1-5: "Therefore, since we have been made right in God's sight by faith, we have peace with God because of what Jesus Christ our Lord has done for us. 2 Because of our faith, Christ has brought us into this place of undeserved privilege where we now stand, and we confidently and joyfully look forward to sharing God's glory" (Rom. 5:1–2, NLT). "3 We also rejoice in our sufferings, because we know that suffering produces perseverance; 4 perseverance, character; and character, hope. 5 And hope does not disappoint us, because God has poured out his love into our hearts by the Holy Spirit, whom he has given us." (Rom. 5:3–5, NIV)

    A. Circle the words "peace" and "hope" in this passage.

    B. What leads to us having peace with God? See Romans 5:1–2.

    C. Starting at Romans 5:3, list the things that build up to "hope."

        1.

        2.

        3.

        4.

    D. Now, let's personalize this a bit. Write one way you feel you've *suffered*, especially because you have a child with special needs.

    E. How has this led you to *persevere*? (*Persevere* is defined as "to maintain a purpose in spite of difficulty, obstacles, or discouragement; continue steadfastly."[16])

    F. How has your perseverance in the midst of suffering led to strength of *character*?

There are several definitions of the word *character*. The Amplified Bible describes it as "approved faith and tried integrity." Here are a few more from dictionary.com: "moral or ethical quality; qualities of honesty, courage, or the like; integrity; an account of the qualities or peculiarities of

---

16 *Dictionary.com Unabridged*, (Random House, Inc. 08 Mar. 2011), <Dictionary.com http://dictionary.reference. com/browse/persevere>.

a person or thing."[17] I love this note on *character* from thesaurus.com, "*character* is what one is; *reputation* is what one is thought to be by others."[18]

    G. Write in capital letters what strength of character leads to: _____!

    H. According to Romans 5:5, why does hope not disappoint us?

Once again, we see God *pouring out* His love into our hearts by the Holy Spirit! God is so very generous in giving good gifts to His children. When we keep our minds and thoughts focused on the Lord, when we trust Him and wait on Him, He faithfully *pours out* His love into our hearts, even in the midst of our pain and sufferings! Because God has poured His love into our hearts, we can have *hope*, a confident expectation that God will work things out for our good and His glory.

3.   Here are two additional verses to reflect upon. "For I know the thoughts and plans that I have for you, says the Lord, thoughts and plans for welfare and peace and not for evil, to give you hope in your final outcome" (Jer. 29:11, Amplified Bible).

"You will guard him and keep him in perfect and constant peace whose mind [both its inclination and its character] is stayed on You, because he commits himself to You, leans on You, and hopes confidently in You" (Isa. 26:3, Amplified Bible).

According to these verses, what gives us hope (that is, confident expectation) for our "final outcome"?

4.   How did the Lord speak to you today?

---

17 *Dictionary.com Unabridged*, (Random House, Inc. 08 Mar. 2011), <Dictionary.com http://dictionary.reference.com/browse/character>.

18 *Roget's 21st Century Thesaurus, Third Edition*, (Philip Lief Group 2009. 08 Mar. 2011), <Thesaurus.com http://thesaurus.com/browse/character>.

WALKING THE JOURNEY

Our therapy appointment today was such a relief, and I am thankful…so very thankful. I've decided I'm not going to talk to anyone else about the counseling session. Our families don't see what life is like when the doors are closed and it is just us with our daughter. And since they don't see it, they don't understand it. Our daughter is very charming and sweet in front of everyone else. They can't see the bad, because she doesn't act like that in front of others. I just can't talk to anyone about Taylor's problems because no one else seems to understand. And for now I need encouragement, not judgment.

Today in our therapy session I learned one thing—and it is a big one. I was so angry at Taylor for her manipulation and for basically being two different people. Then the therapist made me understand that our daughter is not happy and does a lot of negative self-talk. I also learned that she does not enjoy making me miserable, even though it seems like it. Today I saw her as broken, and I needed to see that. I need to try to help her feel better, instead of thinking she is out to destroy me. But I also know that if she doesn't get this help, it will destroy my spirit. I can feel how much this has hurt me over the past five years.

I had such different visions about how it would be, and it has been so hard. I really wasn't prepared for all the unhappiness that everyone would feel with the adoption—including Taylor. I felt like we were doing a good thing, but it has been so painful—not just on me, but on everyone. I'm just really ready to try to make it better instead of giving up. And that was where I have been this school year…just wanting to give up. I am so not a quitter—I don't know why I felt that way!!!!

Today I felt God hearing and answering my prayers that I have been praying for so long.

Lisa's daughter, Taylor, has Reactive Attachment Disorder.

Week 4

Perfect Peace,
Calm Contentment,
Refreshing Rest

"...The LORD turn his face toward you and
give you peace."—Num. 6:26

"'Peace, peace,' they say, when there is no peace" (Jer. 6:14). Do you ever feel like this observation describes your home…your situation? I know the feeling. This is how I feel when my son is unstable and his illness is out of control. I yearn for peace, but at such times there is no peace in our home. We experience all sorts of intense emotions, but *peace* certainly isn't at the top of the list.

So what kind of peace is the apostle Paul talking about when he tells us in Philippians 4:7 that Jesus Christ offers peace that "transcends all understanding"? It must be a peace that has nothing to do with outside circumstances. If we were looking for perfect—and lasting—peace in our circumstances, we would need to live perfect lives and have the people around us live perfect lives as well. And we all know *that's* not going to happen on this side of heaven!

What about contentment? Paul tells us to learn to be content in all situations. Where does this calm contentment come from? Is this something that's available to all of us? Is it really possible to be truly content—even when you have a child with mental illness or severe handicaps?

This week we're going to uncover the treasures of peace, contentment, and rest. We all long for these gifts, don't we? I suspect that in several of our homes we experience a great deal of anger, anxiety, angst, or perhaps worry, fear, and insecurity. But peace, contentment, and rest? Surely life reserves those treasures for parents with healthy and compliant children!

Do you yearn for the kind of peace and rest that Jesus offers? He opens His arms to us and says, "Come to me, all of you who are weary and carry heavy burdens, and I will give you rest. Take my yoke upon you. Let me teach you, because I am humble and gentle at heart, and you will find rest for your souls" (Matt. 11:28–29).

Let's look beyond the circumstances in our lives and discover genuine *peace, contentment, and rest.*

Week 4, Day 1

Kissed by Peace

Peace...so longed for, yet so elusive. We yearn for peace in our hearts and harmony in our homes. People so often talk about peace; they preach about it; they even politicize it. What, really, *is* peace? One Bible dictionary defines it as "a state of tranquility or quiet; harmony in personal relations, especially with God; freedom from disquieting or oppressive thoughts or emotions."[19] How do we reach this "state of tranquility" in the midst of upheaval and upset in our homes? What will lead us to "freedom from oppressive thoughts and emotions" when our minds are racing with worry or agitation? Today and tomorrow we will look closely at the peace that God our Father offers.

The Bible teaches us that in order to have peace with God, with others, and with ourselves, we must first have a right relationship with God.

Please read each passage. Ask God to open the eyes of your heart so that you will understand what He is saying to you.

1. Isa. 32:17: "The fruit of righteousness will be peace; the effect of righteousness will be quietness and confidence forever."

   A. In week three, day five, we coupled "hope and peace" together and saw how they go hand in hand. Today we'll take note of what must be in place before we can experience genuine peace. According to Isaiah 32:17, what must we consume in order to taste peace? "The fruit of _____."

One definition of righteousness is "perfect obedience to God's will and moral standards. God regards us as righteous through Christ if we accept Jesus' sacrifice on our behalf, which takes away the guilt of our disobedience."[20]

It's impossible for us, on our own, to attain the perfect obedience that God's perfect justice requires. Therefore, God sent His Son, Jesus, to be perfectly obedient on our behalf. His sacrifice makes us appear righteous in God's eyes!

---

19   The *Life Application Study Bible*, New Living Translation, Bible Dictionary, Notes and Bible Helps, (Tyndale House Publishers, 1988, 1989, 1990, 1993, 1996, 2004).

20   *Discover Your Bible series, Discover 1 John* (CRC Publications, 2001, Grand Rapids, MI), 9.

B. Is the knowledge that God views you as *righteous* difficult for you to accept? Why or why not?

C. Do your thoughts and actions always reflect your righteousness? Or do you struggle with the "guilt of your disobedience"?

D. How is the guilt of our disobedience taken away?

E. How does the result or the fruit of your righteousness lead to peace, quietness, and confidence?

2. The psalmist cries out, "In my anguish I cried to the LORD, and he answered by setting me free" (Ps. 118:5).

A. How did the Lord respond to the psalmist when he cried out in anguish?

B. From what do you suppose he was "set free"?

C. Have you ever felt the anguish the psalmist is talking about here? Name a time when you cried out to the Lord in pain and anguish, especially about your child.

D. How do you feel the Lord responded to you?

3. Listen to a few other passages from the Psalms. "I will lie down and sleep in peace, for You alone, O LORD, make me dwell in safety" (Ps. 4:8). "But I have stilled and quieted my soul; like a weaned child with its mother, like a weaned child is my soul within me" (Ps. 131:2).

A. How do we see the quiet confidence and peace of the psalmist in these verses?

B. In your situation, what leads to chaos and disruption in your home and heart? (*This is a personal reflection question. You will not need to share this in your group.*)

Now, take a deep breath and close your eyes. Imagine yourself sitting in the arms of your heavenly Father. Spend some time thanking God for His sacrifice on your behalf. Pour out to Him your worries, your anguish, and your tears. Ask Him to soothe your troubled heart. Allow Him to still and quiet your soul. Quietly ask Him to fill you with the effects of righteousness—peace, quietness, and confidence.

4. Read Psalm 85:10: "Love and faithfulness meet together; righteousness and peace kiss each other."

A. Fill in the blanks: "Love and faithfulness _____ together; righteousness and peace _____ each other."

B. What relationship does this bring to mind for you?

This beautiful verse personifies God's intimacy with His children. Can you envision God's love and faithfulness embracing you? Can you imagine God giving you a kiss? Can you feel His righteousness and peace settling over you? What a tender portrayal of God's heart for His much-loved children!

5. Let's close today with a blessing of peace (*shalom*) from the Lord:

    "The LORD bless you and keep you;

    the LORD make his face shine upon you

    and be gracious to you;

    the LORD turn His face toward you

    and give you peace" (Num. 6:24-26).

Shalom is a Hebrew word for peace. It is seen here in its most expressive form—not the absence of war, but a positive state of rightness and well-being. Such peace comes only from God.[21]

6. How did the Lord speak to you today?

---

21   *The NIV Study Bible,* (Zondervan Corporation, 1985), 199.

WALKING THE JOURNEY

It was really hard for me to come back to the hospital. I think I got a taste of normal life and realized how much I missed it. It is so hard to not know how long we will be here. We have had so many setbacks, that even when they do give us a time frame, I don't put a lot of stock in it.

Sometimes I wonder how long we as a family can keep this up. It is taking its toll on all of us. I see changes in Chloe that I have missed while I was gone, and she is more hesitant to be away from us than she was before. My husband and I have good days and bad. So far we have been able to be a support to each other, but at least for me there are still lots of tears. I think we are both grieving the child Anna was before her illness. We don't know how she will be in the future, but no matter what happens, she will be a different child from what she was before. I struggle with all the things she is missing out on and at least for now cannot do.

On my way home Thursday, I listened to a CD of Christian praise songs and cried a lot. It was actually very moving to feel like my heart was broken, but to still at least acknowledge God's majesty and power, even if I didn't feel like praising in a more traditional way. I have moments of anger at God, especially when I feel He is withholding His hand from our situation, but I do not doubt His love. I just doubt His methods. I can't understand how this could be best for Anna or for our family. I know some have said this is a great witness, but sometimes I wish God would use someone else to witness. I just want to be normal. But obviously that isn't part of His plan right now. Someone talked to me about not seeing what is happening in heaven and that makes me feel a little better—that there are things going on that I know nothing about, but God does. I know God is here, but that doesn't take away the pain, fear, loneliness, and discouragement.

Boy, I am really bringing everybody down now. Hopefully by Thursday I can find a little more to be thankful about. Thanks to all who posted. Even if you just say hi or tell me what you did today or what your holiday plans are, I love reading the messages. Please don't feel you have to be "deep." Just say, "Hi! How are you?"

From Julie's Care Pages…

These were Julie's thoughts as she was in the hospital dealing with the sudden and severe illness of her young daughter, Anna. Anna's illness left her permanently disabled. This entry was written after spending some time at home with her other young daughter, Chloe.

Week 4, Day 2

Perfect Peace

Are you feeling embraced and kissed by God's peace yet? Today we'll continue to look intently into God's perfect peace.

Please read each passage. Ask God to open the eyes of your heart so that you will understand what He is saying to you.

1. Isa. 26:3–4: "You will keep in perfect peace him whose mind is steadfast, because he trusts in You. 4 Trust in the LORD forever, for the LORD, the LORD, is the Rock eternal."

   A. To whom does God promise perfect peace?

   B. What do you think "perfect peace" looks like?

   C. Do you ever experience portions of perfect peace in your own life? When do you most often experience this?

   The word *steadfast* is defined as "fixed in direction; firm in purpose; unwavering; firmly fixed in place or position."[22]

   D. Why does the steadfast person experience perfect peace?

   E. What does it mean to you that the Lord is the "Rock eternal"?

2. Phil. 4:5b–7: "The Lord is near. 6 Do not be anxious about anything, but in everything, by prayer and petition, with thanksgiving, present your requests to God. 7 And the peace of God, which transcends all understanding, will guard your hearts and your minds in Christ Jesus."

   I love the way these beautiful words are written in *The Message*. "Don't fret or worry. Instead of worrying, pray. Let petitions and praises shape your worries into prayers, letting God know your concerns. Before you know it, a sense of God's wholeness, everything coming together for good, will come and settle you down. It's wonderful what happens when Christ displaces worry at the center of your life" (Phil. 4:6–7, MSG).

---

22 *Dictionary.com Unabridged*, (Random House, Inc. 08 Mar. 2011), <Dictionary.com http://dictionary.reference.com/browse/steadfast>.

A. About what does God give us permission to be anxious?

B. What are we to turn our worries and fears into?

C. How are we told to present our "prayers and petitions" to God?

D. What does God promise when we do this?

E. How is God's peace defined in Philippians 4:7?

F. What does this kind of peace do for you?

Okay, now that we've taken the text apart and looked at it closely, let's personalize it! First of all, note that the second half of Philippians 4:5 appeared in our reading from the *New International Version*. We can't skip over these four powerful words—"The Lord is near." Do you believe that?

G. What difference does this make to you on those days when you're consumed by worries, anxieties, and fears?

H. We're told in Philippians 4:6 that *everything* can be affected by prayer. What specific worry are you struggling with today, especially regarding your child? Please write it down.

I. Now take that worry and turn it into a prayer. It doesn't need to be eloquent—just honest and sincere. (*This is a personal reflection. You won't be asked to share this in your group.*)

J. Using the text from the NIV, fill in the blanks to be reminded of the work of God's peace. "And the peace of God…will _____ your _____ and _____ in Christ Jesus."

In the U.S. today, the Department of Homeland Security has posted border patrols along our nation's entry points. These soldiers guard our country from the threat of terrorist invasion. The mission statement of CBP (U.S. Customs and Border Protection) defines the agency's purpose this way: "We are the guardians of our nation's borders. We are America's frontline. We safeguard the American homeland at and beyond our borders. We protect the American public against terrorists and the instruments of terror…."[23]

In the same way, God's peace is standing guard at the entry points of our hearts and our minds. When worries, fears, anxieties, and other troublesome thoughts threaten to invade and destroy, we can activate God's peace by turning to Him in prayer. God promises that when we make the choice to pray instead of to worry, He will freely and generously pour His peace into our hearts.

Is this a one-time occurrence? Can we simply pray once and banish our worries forever? Not likely! Just as our country maintains constant guard, so we need to be continuously vigilant. Satan

---

23 "CBP Mission Statement and Core Values," http://www.cbp.gov/xp/cgov/about/mission/guardians.xml.

will not be satisfied to attack us once with worries and fears, and then slink back in defeat. He will try to invade our hearts and minds over and over again.

Don't be discouraged when anxieties and fears start pressing against your sanity five minutes after praying for peace. God is patient with us! He understands. Just go right back to Him, name and confess your worries, and turn them back into prayers. He *will* defend you. He faithfully promises to release His peace into your life.

3. Jesus said to His followers, "I am leaving you with a gift—peace of mind and heart. And the peace I give is a gift the world cannot give. So don't be troubled or afraid" (John 14:27, NLT).

Jesus spoke these comforting words to His disciples shortly before His arrest. He knew His disciples would soon be paralyzed by fear. He also knew they would need this reassurance after His ascension. Jesus promised that His Presence, in the person of the Holy Spirit, would remain with them—and all of His followers—forever.

A. What does Jesus call the kind of peace He gives us?

B. What is a good thing to remember the next time you feel troubled or afraid?

"It's wonderful what happens when Christ displaces worry at the center of your life" (Phil. 4:7, MSG).

4. How did the Lord speak to you today?

WALKING THE JOURNEY

From time to time I like to take a few moments to reflect on how far I've come since I learned that God had chosen us to raise a special needs child. (My husband has always been way ahead of me.)

Year 1:   Denial, anger, despair, drowning in doctor and therapy visits, asking "why me?"

Year 2:   Acceptance, problem solving, prioritizing, new baby.

Year 3:   Love, joy, peace.

Natalie has really started to make her personality known and is really reaching to communicate with us. She's made so much progress in communication during the past six months that we feel certain she will eventually speak. Natalie is so cooperative during therapy and homework that I have to believe she will continue to make great progress. She's trying to run, and her new favorite thing is to play with the basketball.

I guess what I want to share is that I'm more hopeful for the future now than I have been since Natalie was born.

Cindy's daughter was born with a rare disorder that causes mental retardation. This entry was posted on her blog, The Happy Ones. You can access her blog at http://les-heureux.blogspot.com. Used with permission.

Week 4, Day 3

Contentment—A Heart at Peace

When our heart is not at peace, we discover this leads to another symptom of unrest—a lack of contentment. It's easy to get caught up in the comparison game. We compare our marriages, our families, our wealth, our material goods, our careers, our homes, and so on, with the lives of others. If our comparisons reveal us falling short, we become jealous and discontent. I believe that parents of special needs children especially struggle with this temptation. When we compare our children with "normal" kids and our families with theirs, our bruised hearts become a breeding ground for discontent. Let's go to the Word for some healing.

Please read each passage. Ask God to open the eyes of your heart so that you will understand what He is saying to you.

1. Prov. 14:30 (NLT): "A peaceful heart leads to a healthy body; jealousy is like cancer in the bones."

   A. To what does a peaceful heart lead?

   B. To what is jealousy compared?

   The word "cancer," in its most common use, is defined as a "malignant and invasive growth." The word 'malignant' is an adjective used to describe a "very dangerous or harmful influence or effect." It is "disposed to cause harm, suffering, or distress *deliberately*" (italics mine).[24]

   In days one and two, we established that a heart at peace is a gift from the Lord...a result of turning our worries into prayers and steadfastly trusting God.

   C. Reread Proverbs 14:30. Where (who) do you suppose the "jealousy cancer" comes from?

   D. When left untreated, cancer spreads throughout the body damaging organs and eventually causing death. In your opinion, what happens when the "jealousy cancer" is left untreated?

2. The Apostle Paul writes in Philippians 4:11b–13, "I have learned to be content whatever the circumstances. 12 I know what it is to be in need, and I know what it is to have plenty.

---

24 *Dictionary.com Unabridged*, (Random House, Inc. 08 Mar. 2011), <Dictionary.com http://dictionary.reference. com/browse/malignant>.

I have learned the secret of being content in any and every situation, whether well fed or hungry, whether living in plenty or in want. 13 I can do everything through Him who gives me strength."

   A. Do you suppose the Apostle Paul was *born* content? Fill in the blanks. "I have _____ to be content whatever the circumstances…. I have _____ the secret of being content…."

God sent Paul on some incredibly difficult field trips to learn the secret of true and lasting contentment.

   B. According to Paul in Philippians 4:13, what is the secret to contentment? Rewrite his answer here.

   C. In what areas of your life do you especially struggle with a lack of contentment? (*This is a personal reflection question. You will not need to share this in your group.*)

If left untreated, the sin of envy will become like a dangerous cancer rotting your bones. Please spend some time confessing these jealousies to the Lord, drawing on His power for the strength you need. Ask the Lord to remove these envious desires from your heart and to teach you contentment in every circumstance.

3. Ps. 16:5–6: "LORD, you have assigned me my portion and my cup;

You have made my lot secure.

6 The boundary lines have fallen for me in pleasant places;

surely I have a delightful inheritance."

   A. Who assigned us our "portion and cup"? Who makes our "lot secure"?

   B. How would you define your portion…your cup…your lot?

   C. Several other versions of the Bible put a slightly different slant on Ps. 16:5. Read this verse in these versions:

- New Living Translation: "Lord, you alone are my inheritance, my cup of blessing. You guard all that is mine."

- Amplified Bible: "The Lord is my chosen and assigned portion, my cup; You hold and maintain my lot."

- New King James Version: "O LORD, *You are* the portion of my inheritance and my cup; You maintain my lot."

- Contemporary English Version: "You, LORD, are all I want! You are my choice, and you keep me safe."

D. *Who* is our portion and cup?

E. What reassurance do we get from the Lord regarding our "lot," meaning all that is ours? Fill in the blanks from the various translations.

　　1. NIV: "Lord, you have assigned me my portion and my cup; You have made my lot _____."

　　2. NLT: "Lord, you alone are my inheritance, my cup of blessing. You _____ all that is mine."

　　3. AMP: "The Lord is my chosen and assigned portion, my cup; You _____ and _____ my lot."

　　4. NKJV: "O LORD, *You are* the portion of my inheritance and my cup; You _____ my lot."

　　5. CEV: "You, LORD, are all I want! You are my choice, and you _____ me _____."

F. How can we testify, with the Psalmist, that "the boundary lines have fallen for me in pleasant places," even when we're struggling with the challenges of a special needs child?

G. As believers, what "delightful inheritance" can we anticipate?

4. How did the Lord speak to you today?

WALKING THE JOURNEY

School is underway again and unfortunately it's not been a great start to the year. Kyle's anxiety is in full bloom. His final words to me tonight were, "I'm *not* going to school anymore." (Sigh.) Tomorrow morning could be a little dicey (typical).

I'm a member of an online support group for parents of adolescents and teens with bipolar disorder. Tonight someone sent a blog that she found meaningful. It was about letting go of your mind and body through yoga. She talked about centering herself...letting go of the pain...releasing and relaxing the body and mind...trusting. She finds yoga helpful when her child's world (and therefore her own) is spinning out of control because of her child's illness.

I found the blog interesting—especially the timing of it. When Kyle is unstable, we all feel the effects. To be honest, it's been a difficult week. It takes a lot of strength to not be sucked down into the swirling vortex of the emotions of mental illness. So what is there to hold onto? What can I do to regain some equilibrium; to bring my mind and body back to a place of peace when there's anger, anxiety, and agitation all around me? Is yoga the answer? I question that. Nowhere in her blog did the author write about who or what she is trusting, once she "lets go." She simply empties her mind. But what will fill her mind once it's emptied? What happens when her daughter wakes up tomorrow still angry with the world...still unstable...still ill? What good does an "empty mind" do then?

God led me to a beautiful prayer this week. I just finished reading Brennan Manning's book, *The Ragamuffin Gospel*. He suggests a "prayer of simple regard." Simply breathe in and out as you pray, "Abba...I belong to You." As you do this, you become filled with such a profound awareness of who you are and to Whom you belong. It's such a comfort to be reminded with every breath you breathe that One much stronger than you is in control of each crazy situation you encounter.

Even though my world sometimes feels as if it's spinning out of control, God assures me it's not. When I empty myself of me—when I let go and trust my Abba—God fills my mind with incredible peace. And Abba Father's peace exceeds anything the world offers.

An excerpt from my blog during Kyle's senior year. You can access my blog at http://bevroozeboom. blogspot.com.

Week 4, Day 4

"Come to Me..."

Do you ever struggle with overwhelming weariness? Today we're going to listen to the call of Jesus. He looks at us with gentle, understanding eyes, extends His hands to us and tenderly beckons us to *come....*

Please read each passage. Ask God to open the eyes of your heart so that you will understand what He is saying to you.

1. Matt. 11:28–30: "Then Jesus said, "Come to me, all of you who are weary and carry heavy burdens, and I will give you rest. 29 Take my yoke upon you. Let me teach you, because I am humble and gentle at heart, and you will find rest for your souls. 30 For my yoke is easy to bear, and the burden I give you is light."

    A. What beautiful invitation is Jesus extending here?

    B. To whom is He extending it?

    C. Do you feel weary? What heavy burdens are you carrying today?

    D. What instructions do we receive in Matthew 11:29?

How does taking on the yoke of Jesus help us with our heavy burdens? A "yoke" is a device that joins together a pair of draft animals, especially oxen. In this passage, Jesus is saying, "Step into my yoke, and we'll pull the plow across the field together." Too often we try to shoulder our burdens alone. It's hard to ask others for help, so we just tough it out. Unfortunately, this attitude often carries over into our relationship with the Lord as well. He stands ready and willing to help carry our burdens, but we don't allow Him to help shoulder our load. How much easier it would be for us if we would allow Jesus to step into the role of lead ox, to submit to His leading and His will.

    E. Do you ever feel like the Lord is leading you in a direction you do not want to go? Explain.

    F. In what areas of your child's life do you find yourself wrestling for control?

G. What promises are we given in these verses? Highlight or underline each promise, then write it here.

The fuller intent and deeper meaning of this passage is that Jesus invites us to come to Him with the burden and weight of our sin. Jesus promises that when we acknowledge and repent of our sin, He gives us the free gift of salvation. We can find "rest for our souls" in the promise that our salvation is secure in Him. Jesus does not place a heavy yoke of "dos and don'ts" on our shoulders. The yoke that Jesus places on us is His unfailing love and all-encompassing peace.

H. What kind of "burden" are we given, according to Matthew 11:30?

Listen to what the *Believer's Bible Commentary* says about this verse: "This does not mean that there are no problems, trials, labor, or heartaches in the Christian life. But it does mean that we do not have to bear them alone. We are yoked with the One who gives sufficient grace for every time of need. To serve Him is not bondage but perfect freedom."[25]

I. How do you sense the Lord helping you bear the load of your child and his or her challenges? List as many ways as you can think of.

2. Ps. 62:5–8: "Find rest, O my soul, in God alone;

my hope comes from Him.

6 He alone is my rock and my salvation;

He is my fortress, I will not be shaken.

7 My salvation and my honor depend on God;

He is my mighty rock, my refuge.

8 Trust in Him at all times, O people;

pour out your hearts to Him,

for God is our refuge."

A. According to Psalm 62:5, who is the only source of true rest?

B. List all the ways God is described in these verses.

C. Fill in the blanks from Psalm 62:8. "＿＿＿＿＿＿ in Him at ＿＿＿ times, O people; ＿＿＿＿＿＿ out your ＿＿＿＿＿＿ to Him, for God is our ＿＿＿＿＿＿."

D. The word "trust" here literally means to "attach yourself to Him." How would attaching ourselves to the Lord lead to rest for our souls (See Psalm 62:5.)?

3. In Exodus 33:14, we read what God said to Moses before leading the Israelites to the Promised Land. "The LORD replied, 'My Presence will go with you, and I will give you rest.'"

---

25 William MacDonald; *Believer's Bible Commentary,* (Thomas Nelson Publishers, Inc., Nashville, TN, 1995, 1992, 1990, 1989), 1246, 1247.

A. What two promises did God make to Moses?

    1.

    2.

B. What is God's promise to you in this verse?

4. How did the Lord speak to you today?

WALKING THE JOURNEY

It is the hardest thing as a mother not to know what is wrong and be able to fix it. This was one of the hardest nights so far for me, because Anna was so upset, and I can't get upset or at least I can't show it. I am even feeling guilty right now because I am down the hall, but after she finally went to sleep, I just could not take that room any more.

I know that God is here, but it is so hard to understand His ways at times. I really feel right now like I am in the pit that David talks about in the Psalms. I was feeling so good yesterday and now another setback. Even though my brain knows this is not forever, my spirit is sunk. I just trust that God will bring us through even when I cannot feel His presence. Please pray a lot for us today. I am feeling like I don't know how many more crises I can take and still be here for her. Please pray for strength for me and for comfort for Anna. Also pray for my husband as he is home and at work, and that must be so hard. Please pray for a special blessing for us today, whatever form it may take.

I feel like I need something from God to get me through. I know He will not give me more than I can handle, but right now I feel like He got my file mixed up with someone else's, like Mother Theresa.

An entry from Julie's Care Pages sharing her thoughts as she was in the hospital dealing with the sudden and severe illness of her young daughter —an illness which left her daughter permanently disabled.

Week 4, Day 5

Strength for the Weary

This week we've been focusing on *peace*; looking closely at what a heart at peace looks like. Yesterday and today we're centering our attention on the aspect of *rest* —something we all need and long for, especially when our burdens get heavy. We saw yesterday that Jesus invites us to slip our shoulders under His yoke and to allow Him to carry the bulk of our load. When we attach ourselves to Him, we will find rest for our souls. Today we're going to delight in the assurance that Jesus not only invites us to come under His yoke, He also promises to give *strength to the weary*. So…pour yourself a cup of tea, put your feet up, and bask in His promises!

1. Isa. 40:25–31:

   "To whom will you compare me?

   Or who is my equal?" says the Holy One.

   26 Lift your eyes and look to the heavens:

   Who created all these?

   He who brings out the starry host one by one,

   and calls them each by name.

   Because of his great power and mighty strength,

   not one of them is missing.

   27 Why do you say, O Jacob,

   and complain, O Israel,

   "My way is hidden from the LORD;

   my cause is disregarded by my God"?

   28 Do you not know?

   Have you not heard?

   The LORD is the everlasting God,

   the Creator of the ends of the earth.

   He will not grow tired or weary,

   and his understanding no one can fathom.

29 He gives strength to the weary

  and increases the power of the weak.

30 Even youths grow tired and weary,

  and young men stumble and fall;

31 but those who hope in the LORD

  will renew their strength.

  They will soar on wings like eagles;

  they will run and not grow weary,

  they will walk and not be faint.

A. Ask yourself, first of all, is anyone the Lord's equal? How does this passage refute this position?

B. What is the Lord saying in Isaiah 40:27?

C. Do you carry *any* burden or sorrow that is "hidden from the Lord" or "disregarded by God"?

D. How does the prophet describe God in Isaiah 40:28?

E. List some parts of God's creation.

Psalm 104 is a beautiful Psalm about creation. This Psalm reminds us not only that God creates, but also that He maintains, preserves, and governs His creation. Listen to how these verses remind us of God's sovereignty over all creation:

- Ps. 104:5: "He set the earth on its foundations; it can never be moved."

- Ps. 104:9: "You set a boundary they (the waters) cannot cross; never again will they cover the earth."

- Ps. 104:19–23: "The moon marks off the seasons, and the sun knows when to go down…it becomes night, and all the beasts of the forest prowl…The sun rises, and they steal away…man goes out to his work until evening."

- Ps. 104:27–28: "These all look to You and You give them their food at the proper time…when You open Your hand, they are satisfied with good things."

F. If God's power is sufficient to handle this whole universe, do you think His power is sufficient to handle your life?

G. Look at Psalm 104:27–28 and then fill in the blanks. "These all look to You and _____ _____ them their food at the proper time…when You _____ Your _____, they are satisfied with good things."

Did you catch from this psalm how personally God relates to His creation? He hand-feeds the animals! God is all-powerful, but He is also all-personal. He loves us and cares for each one of us individually. If He takes such good care of the wild animals, don't you think He'll meet our needs as well?

H. Look again at the passage from Isaiah 40 earlier in today's reading. Fill in the blanks, using Isaiah 40:28 as your guide. "He will _____ grow _____ or _____, and His _____ no one can fathom."

I. Describe the last time you felt bone-tired, completely devoid of strength. What caused the weariness? Was it a physical weariness, emotional weariness, or both?

J. Have you ever wondered if God is ever just too tired—or too distracted—to listen to you, to help you, or to provide for you? Is He really?

K. According to Isaiah 40:29, from where does our strength and power come?

I love how the *NIV Life Application Bible* fleshes out these verses: "Even the strongest people get tired at times, but God's power and strength never diminish. He is never too tired or too busy to help and listen. His strength is our source of strength. When you feel all of life crushing you and cannot go another step, remember that you can call upon God to renew your strength."[26]

L. What does it mean to you that God's strength and energy never diminish, never drain away?

M. Look at Isaiah 40:31. Find the amazing promises given in this verse. "Those who hope in the Lord...":

will _____ their strength;

will _____ on wings like eagles;

will _____ and not grow weary;

will _____ and not be faint.

An eagle flies by spreading its wings and soaring on updrafts and thermals. It can go for miles by simply opening its wings and coasting on the air currents. What an incredible image for us! When we put our hope in the Lord, He promises to renew our strength. He will be the wind under our wings...our source of strength and power. When we place our trust in the Lord, He promises to lift us above the demands and the difficulties of our day. We can rest in Him.

Spend a few minutes opening your arms to Him. Picture yourself floating on His gentle air. Let Him be your strength, your energy. The next time your life spins out of control, take a few

---

26 The *Life Application Study Bible,* New International Version edition, (Tyndale House Publishers, 1988, 1989, 1990, 1991), 1235.

seconds to recall this sensation. Relish these promises and the One in whose strength you can depend. Feel Him lifting you above the franticness—above the noise.

2. Psalm 119:28 reminds us, "My soul is weary with sorrow; strengthen me according to Your word." The *Amplified Bible* presents the verse this way: "My life dissolves and weeps itself away for heaviness; raise me up and strengthen me according to [the promises of] Your word."

   A. Think about a time when you experienced being "weary with sorrow," days when you felt like your soul, your life, and your essence were "dissolving and weeping with heaviness." What did these emotions look like? What were you experiencing?

   B. Where can we go for strength? Where will we find God's beautiful promises for us?

3. How did the Lord speak to you today?

WALKING THE JOURNEY

Welcome to Holland

I am often asked to describe the experience of raising a child with a disability to try to help people who have not shared that unique experience to understand it, to imagine how it would feel. It's like this....

When you're going to have a baby, it's like planning a fabulous vacation trip to Italy. You buy a bunch of guidebooks and make your wonderful plans: the Coliseum, Michelangelo's David, and the gondolas in Venice. You may learn some handy phrases in Italian. It's all very exciting.

After months of eager anticipation, the day finally arrives. You pack your bags and off you go. Several hours later, the plane lands. The stewardess comes in and says, "Welcome to Holland."

"Holland?!" you say. "What do you mean Holland? I signed up for Italy! I'm supposed to be in Italy. All my life I've dreamed of going to Italy."

But there's been a change in the flight plan. They've landed in Holland and there you must stay.

The important thing is that they haven't taken you to a horrible, disgusting, filthy place, full of pestilence, famine, and disease. It's just a different place.

So you must go out and buy new guidebooks. And you must learn a whole new language. And you will meet a whole new group of people you would never have met.

It's just a different place. It's slower-paced than Italy, less flashy than Italy. But after you've been there for a while and you catch your breath, you look around you and you begin to notice that Holland has windmills—and Holland has tulips. Holland even has Rembrandts.

But everyone you know is busy coming and going from Italy...and they're all bragging about what a wonderful time they had there. And for the rest of your life, you will say, "Yes, that's where I was supposed to go. That's what I had planned."

And the pain will never, ever, ever, ever go away, because the loss of that dream is a very, very significant loss.

But if you spend your life mourning the fact that you didn't get to Italy, you may never be free to enjoy the very special, the very lovely things about Holland.

By Emily Perl Kingsley

—Welcome to Holland: Parenting a Special Needs child. http://www.specialkidstoday.com/articles/essays/welcome-to-holland-4719/2/

WEEK 5

Living the Abundant Life

"The thief comes only in order to steal, kill, and destroy. I came so that everyone would enjoy life, and have it in abundance."—John 10:10

INTRODUCTION

Over the past four weeks, we've been reminded that God keeps His *promises* and we've immersed ourselves in His *unfailing love.* We've seen that God is on our side and that nothing can separate us from His lavish love.

We've learned that we can *trust* God. God truly is who He says He is. We've seen that God is bigger than our challenges and burdens.

We've also been reminded of the *hope and assurance* we have for today and for our future. We've seen that Christ alone offers the *peace, contentment, and rest* that we so long for and desire.

This week we're going to come face to face with another incredible promise in Scripture. God's Word assures us that *He equips those whom He calls!* God has surely called us to be mothers of children with special needs. We don't dispute that any longer. But how has He equipped us? What weapons are available to us and how do we get them? And how do these weapons enable us to live the abundant life God promises?

God assures us that He has given us two powerful weapons to battle the giants we face: His Word and prayer. The words of Ephesians 6:10, 17–18 exhort us, "Be strong in the Lord and in His mighty power. Take…the sword of the Spirit, which is the Word of God. And pray in the Spirit on all occasions with all kinds of prayers and requests."

This week we are going to unlock one more treasure the Lord has in store for us…an abundant, fruitful life—a life fully equipped to carry out our calling! To discover this treasure, we'll eagerly ignite those two powerful sticks of dynamite: His Word and prayer!

Week 5, Day 1

Called by the Lord...
Equipped for His Purposes

As I write this final week of study, my son faces partial hospitalization for outpatient treatment. Do I see it as a coincidence? No. I know that God's timing is perfect and that He has so much to teach me. I still struggle with finding joy in my daily life while my son is unstable. I long to live the "abundant life," but often find myself worrying that somehow I'm missing the mark.

Life can be bleak when mental illness rears its ugly head in our home. But it's precisely in the midst of trials like these that Christ calls us to abundant life. We can enjoy our life today—even when we're facing huge struggles. But we need to stay connected to the Word. His Word is alive and active and overflowing with hope!

Please read each passage. Ask God to open the eyes of your heart so that you will understand what He is saying to you.

1. John 10:10: Jesus said, "The thief comes only to steal and kill and destroy; I have come that they may have life, and have it to the full."

    A. Who is the thief?

    B. What is the thief's purpose?

    C. Why did Jesus come?

    The New Living Translation tells us that Jesus came to give us a "rich and satisfying life." The New King James Version uses those beautiful words with which we are so familiar: "I have come that they may have life, and that they may have it more abundantly."

    D. What do you think "life to the full" or an "abundant life" looks like?

    I like the way the *Believer's Bible Commentary* states it. "We receive life the moment we accept Him as our Savior. After we are saved, however, we find that there are various degrees of enjoyment of this life. The more we turn ourselves over to the Holy Spirit, the more we enjoy the life which has been given to us. We not only have *life* then, but we have it more abundantly."[27]

The Good Shepherd searches for His sheep. He calls us to follow Him. Then He equips us for our unique tasks.

2. 2 Chron. 16:9: "For the eyes of the LORD range throughout the earth to strengthen those whose hearts are fully committed to Him."

    A. For whom is the Lord searching?

    B. Why?

According to thesaurus.com, one of the definitions of the word *strengthen* is to "encourage, hearten." Some of the synonyms include "back up, brace, carry weight, embolden, enliven, fortify, rejuvenate, restore, uphold...."[28]

    C. When you look back at your past, specifically with your child, how have you felt the Lord strengthening you?

3. Ps. 4:3: "Know that the LORD has set apart the godly for Himself; the LORD will hear when I call to Him."

    A. Whom has the Lord chosen to be His very own?

    B. How would you define "godly"?

Do we need to be *perfect* for God to view us as godly? No. God considers us godly when we place our trust in Him and are faithful and devoted to Him. We can be assured that, as believers, we have been set apart by God. He has chosen us as His very own and He loves us completely!

    C. What promises do we receive in this verse?

4. 2 Peter 1:3–4: "His divine power has given us everything we need for life and godliness through our knowledge of Him who called us by His own glory and goodness. 4 Through these He has given us His very great and precious promises, so that through them you may participate in the divine nature and escape the corruption in the world caused by evil desires."

For each verse below, fill in the blanks.

---

27 William McDonald; *Believer's Bible Commentary* (Thomas Nelson Publishers, Inc., Nashville, TN, 1995, 1992, 1990, 1989), 1525.

28 *Roget's 21st Century Thesaurus, Third Edition*, (Philip Lief Group 2009, 08 Mar. 2011), <Thesaurus.com http://thesaurus.com/browse/strengthen>.

A. What has God's "divine power" given us? "His divine power has given us _____ _____ _____ for _____ and _____...."

B. How do we know of this divine power? Please finish 2 Peter 1:3. "Through our _____ of _____ who has called us by His own glory and goodness."

C. What has God's "glory and goodness" revealed to us? "Through these He has given us His very _____ and _____ _____...."

D. What do these great and precious promises enable us to participate in and escape from? "...so that through them you may participate in the _____ _____ and escape the _____ in the world caused by evil desires."

God has pursued and chosen *you* to be the mother of your precious child! Yes, it's a daunting task, one that often seems impossible. But He has promised to give you everything you need to do the job—and to do it well. *Those whom God calls, He also equips.*

It is immensely important for us to abide in His Word. We must have personal knowledge of the One who has called us. If we just scratch the surface of His Word, we will miss so much. How can we have an intimate, personal relationship with the Lord if we never spend time with Him, never listen to Him, or never speak to Him? God invites us to share His divine nature. He desires that His nature would become part of us. It's almost incomprehensible! What an amazing promise!

Are you ready to receive "everything you need for life and godliness"? Will you open your arms to receive His divine power? Your response begins as simply as sitting still before the Lord and opening your heart to receive His promises as you read His precious words. We must abide with Him....

5. How did the Lord speak to you today?

WALKING THE JOURNEY

I am so down this morning. I have a lot of pain in my heart when I think of my son going to partial hospitalization. It's a relief in a sense (getting help for our son), but also very sad. It's not even in the ballpark of how you plan to spend the first few weeks of summer. I'm sad for what he's missing in life. I'm sad for what my husband and I are missing. I wish my son could play ball, hang out with friends, work, and just love summer. I wish he could go to camps and Serve projects and start dating. He's being denied all of these things, and in a way, so are we. Our days are filled with anger, impatience, anxiety. Hiding and seeking. Bargaining. Bribing. Threats. I just want a happy, carefree sixteen-year-old boy.

These were my thoughts on the summer morning we admitted our son to partial hospitalization.

WEEK 5, DAY 2

ATTACHED TO THE VINE

Yesterday we learned an important truth: *those whom God calls, He equips.* He has called you—chosen you—to be the mom of a child with special needs and challenges, and He has equipped you for this job! But how do we receive this equipping? When we become believers, God pours His Holy Spirit into our hearts and lives. The beautiful words of 2 Peter 1:3 (see question 4 from yesterday's lesson for a review) assure us that "His divine power has given us *everything we need* for life and godliness…." So how are we energized by this divine power? How do we tap into it so that we don't become dried up and dusty, especially in the daily demands of our lives? We do this by being attached to Christ the Vine…by abiding.

Please read each passage. Ask God to open the eyes of your heart so that you will understand what He is saying to you.

1. John 10:3–4: "…The sheep listen to His voice. He calls His sheep by name and leads them out…His sheep follow Him because they know His voice." John 10:14: "I am the Good Shepherd; I know my sheep and my sheep know me…." John 10:27: "My sheep listen to my voice; I know them and they follow me…."

   A. Who is the Good Shepherd? Who are the sheep?

   B. Fill in the blanks, using John 10:3–4 as a guide. "The sheep _____ to his voice. He calls his sheep _____ _____ and leads them out."

   C. How well does the Good Shepherd know His sheep?

   D. How well do the sheep know their Shepherd?

   Do you spend time with the Good Shepherd? How well do you know Him? Do you recognize His voice when He speaks? Do you understand His compassion, feel His touch, perceive His authority, and see His light in the darkness? Do you believe He loves you even more than you love your own children? *Is it your heart's desire to become more and more like Jesus?* How are we to do this?

2. John 15:4: Jesus said, "Remain in me, and I will remain in you. No branch can bear fruit by itself; it must remain in the vine. Neither can you bear fruit unless you remain in me." The New King James Version presents the same verse like this: "Abide in Me, and I in you. As

the branch cannot bear fruit of itself, unless it abides in the vine, neither can you, unless you abide in Me."

A. What are we told to do in this passage?

According to dictionary.com, *abide* means "to stay; to continue in a place; to wait for; to be prepared for." Some synonyms of the word *abide* are "continue, endure, keep on, last, persevere."[29]

B. Looking at this definition, what do you think it means to "remain" or "abide" in the vine and how are we to do this?

C. If you cut a branch from a grape vine, how many grapes would you expect that branch to yield? Why is this?

D. To what kind of fruit bearing does Jesus call us, especially as moms of special needs kids?

3. Ps: 43:3: "Send forth Your light and Your truth,

let them guide me;

let them bring me to Your holy mountain,

to the place where You dwell."

A. What was the Psalmist asking God to do?

B. What situation are you facing now, especially with your child, through which you long for God's light and truth to guide you?

Turn this Psalm into your own personal prayer! Abide with the Lord for a while and sit at His feet. Ask Him to chase away the darkness, the weakness, the feelings of inadequacy with which you struggle. Ask Him to guide you with His truth; then follow where He leads.

4. Ps. 119:105: "Your word is a lamp to my feet and a light for my path."

A. How does the psalmist describe God's Word in this verse?

When we walk into a dark room, especially one that's unfamiliar, the first thing we do is turn on a light. We know that if we don't, we're liable to trip over something and possibly hurt ourselves. In the same way, if we don't open God's Word, meditate on it, and abide in it, we're closing ourselves off from the power and light that's available to us. When we find ourselves in dark and unfamiliar territory (i.e. raising a child with special needs), we would be wise to turn on the Light! This little verse packs such huge promises. God's "lamp to my feet" promises light

---

29 *Dictionary.com Unabridged*. Random House, Inc. 08 Mar. 2011. <Dictionary.com http://dictionary.reference. com/browse/abide>.

for the step I'm taking right now, and God's "light for my path" promises light for my immediate future!

    B. Do you spend time each day meditating on God's Word? Is God inviting you to abide more deeply? (*This is a personal reflection question. You won't be asked to share this in your group.*)

5.   How did the Lord speak to you today?

Walking the Journey

Here are some ways to make a conscious effort to spend time with God and to meditate on His Word each day. These are especially helpful for moms who have a difficult time carving out a "quiet time" with the Lord in the midst of the many demands placed upon them.

1. Make liberal use of index cards! When you come across a verse that God seems to have written just for you, write it on an index card. Tape it to your bathroom mirror, kitchen cupboards, or above the changing table and read it as often as possible. Meditate on the same Scripture verse for several days. Ask the Lord what message He has for you in that verse. Practice memorizing!

2. Use whatever quiet time you have in your day as a divine appointment to meet with God.

3. Talk to God out loud whenever possible—when you're in the shower, alone in the car, on a walk, jogging, or vacuuming the floors. Be aware of His presence and engage Him in dialogue!

4. Enjoy the gift of music! Play praise songs in your van as you carpool across town, sing and dance to praise and worship songs with your kids at home, softly play instrumental music in your quiet times (this is especially meaningful while praying), turn on music to help pass the time while folding laundry, cleaning the house, and paying the bills.

5. Download messages from your favorite pastors or speakers and listen to them at your convenience.

6. Sign up for an online devotional. Every morning when you check your e-mail you'll have a word of encouragement waiting for you!

7. Pray breath prayers—short sentence prayers—as they come to your mind during the day. Pray about anything and anyone at anytime and anyplace!

8. Be aware of when you're feeling anxious. Turn your worries into a prayer.

9. Get into the habit of praying out loud with your children.

10. Before you fall asleep at night, ask God to wake you up in the morning so that you can spend some meaningful time together with Him before your kids wake up.

GOD'S WORD...
OUR SWORD, OUR SHIELD, OUR TREASURE

The writer of Ephesians calls God's Word the sword of the Spirit. This wording implies that God's Word is a weapon. What does it look like to hold this weapon in our grip? What power is available to us and just how do we get it?

Today we'll see that God's Word is not only a weapon, it is also our defense. It is our flawless, perfect shield...one in which we can take refuge when we are facing battles against dedicated opposition. We will also learn that God's Word is a treasure. When we open it, we will discover an abundance of riches!

Please read each passage. Ask God to open the eyes of your heart so that you will understand what He is saying to you.

1. Ps. 18:28–32: "You, O LORD, keep my lamp burning;

   my God turns my darkness into light.

   29 With Your help I can advance against a troop;

   with my God I can scale a wall.

   30 As for God, His way is perfect;

   the word of the LORD is flawless.

   He is a shield

   for all who take refuge in Him.

   31 For who is God besides the LORD?

   And who is the Rock except our God?

   32 It is God who arms me with strength

   and makes my way perfect."

   A. Who keeps our "lamp burning" and turns our "darkness into light"?

   B. What power are we given, according to Psalm 18:29?

I love the imagery of this verse! In my mind's eye, I see myself morph into some sort of superhero standing against powerful foes and scaling walls (with the ability "to leap tall buildings in a single bound!"). But when we look at these verses a little more closely, we see that the power doesn't rest with us at all.

C. Who must we have on our side to help us fight our battles? Fill in the blanks to see the references in these verses.

"_____, O _____ keep my lamp burning; _____ _____ turns my darkness into light. With _____ help I can advance against a troop; with my _____ I can scale a wall. As for _____, His way is perfect; the word of the LORD is flawless. _____ is a shield for all who take refuge in _____. For who is _____ beside the LORD? And who is the _____ except our God? It is _____ who arms me with strength and makes my way perfect."

Are we superheroes in our own strength? Absolutely not!!

2. Ps: 18:33–36: "He makes my feet like the feet of a deer;

   He enables me to stand on the heights.

   34 He trains my hands for battle;

   my arms can bend a bow of bronze.

   35 You give me Your shield of victory, and Your right hand sustains me;

   You stoop down to make me great.

   36 You broaden the path beneath me,

   so that my ankles do not turn."

   A. These verses follow the previous ones we just studied. When we're facing a battle of any kind, how does God strengthen us? Fill in the blanks.

   "He makes my _____ like the feet of a _____;

   He enables me to _____ on the heights.

   He _____ my _____ for battle;

   You give me _____ _____ of victory;

   _____ right hand sustains me;

   _____ stoop down to make _____ great.

   _____ broaden the path beneath me, so that _____ ankles do not turn."

   B. Does God promise to *eliminate* the challenges and difficulties in our lives?

   C. What does God promise us when we're faced with seemingly insurmountable problems?

God will never leave us alone to fight the giants we face in our lives. He promises to stand beside us, to teach us, and to strengthen us. We need to abide in Him and find refuge in His arms. We do this is by storing God's Word in our hearts.

3. Prov. 2:1–6: "My child, if you accept My words and store up My commands within you, 2 turning your ear to wisdom and applying your heart to understanding, 3 and if you call out for insight and cry aloud for understanding, 4 and if you look for it as for silver and search for it as for hidden treasure, 5 then you will understand the fear of the LORD and find the knowledge of God. 6 For the LORD gives wisdom, and from His mouth come knowledge and understanding."

   A. What (Who) is the source of true wisdom, knowledge, and understanding?

   B. What are we to do with God's words and commands?

   C. (*These are personal reflection questions. You won't be asked to share your answers with your group.*) What questions do you have hidden deep in your heart…questions you dare only whisper to the Lord on the darkest night? Are you struggling to understand why God gave you a child with a mental or physical illness? Are you despairing because your marriage is on the rocks due to the pressure and stress you deal with every day? Do you wonder where God is and why He's allowing so much junk to come into your life?

I would encourage you to spend time each day digging into God's Word, meditating on His promises, and calling out to Him for insight and understanding. God *promises* to give wisdom, knowledge, and understanding to all who sincerely cry out to Him. Perhaps God will fully explain His will and purposes to you (but oftentimes He may not—remember Job?), but most *definitely* God will bring you closer to His heart, to a deeper level of love and faith, and a more complete understanding of just who is your Abba and how very much He loves you.

4. Isa. 33:6: "He will be the sure foundation for your times, a rich store of salvation and wisdom and knowledge; the fear of the LORD is the key to this treasure."

   A. How does Isaiah describe the Lord in this passage?

   B. What treasure does His "rich store" yield?

   C. What is the key to this treasure?

The fear of the Lord is the key to the treasure we seek. I have prayed that as you've gone through these past five weeks, you have reached a deeper understanding of what God does and does not promise. He does *not* promise us a life of ease. (I know I don't have to spell that out for you who are reading this book. Your life is anything but easy!) But God does promise that when we sincerely search for Him—seek Him with all of our heart—He *will* be our sure foundation! He *will* enable our feet to stand on the heights! He *will* help us scale walls and face foes, no matter what form they take. His Words of promise will become like treasures of silver and gold for us as we go through our days.

5. How did the Lord speak to you today?

WALKING THE JOURNEY

So our lives have been stressful and crazy, but it is getting better. I have been trying to pray a lot and depend on God day by day. Easier said than done. It has been a long journey for God and me the last few months. I think anyone who goes through something like this goes through a time of questioning who God is and how He works. At least that is true for me. I still don't understand all of that, but I feel like God is answering my questions as I ask. He is speaking to me through His word and a Bible study I've been doing and through Christian friends.

I do feel like God is good, and He is in control, although I do not like where He has taken us. I know that if I keep trying to honestly understand God's character, He will reward my search. I pray that as Anna grows, she will be able to search for God and His character in her own way. I really believe that God does not expect us to understand everything, just to keep searching and trust in His character as we do. Anna will have to search as well and find her own answers, but I know that God will be faithful to her search—as He has been to mine.

I thank all of you who have prayed for our family through our physical struggles as well as our emotional and spiritual struggles. It is so wonderful to have brothers and sisters praying for us when we don't have the strength to pray.

From Julie's Care Pages as her family neared the end of Anna's hospital stay. Anna's illness left her permanently disabled.

Week 5, Day 4

Lord, Teach us to Pray!

Over the past three days, we've looked at how God has chosen us, called us, and equipped us for His purposes. We received reminders that His divine power has given us everything we need to carry out our calling. We saw that we must remain attached to the Vine. We must allow the Word of God to sink deep into our hearts, so that we can recognize the voice of our Shepherd and follow His calling. We were reminded that God's Word is a light, a lamp, a shield, and a treasure. What amazing power is available to those who tap into it! Christ is the "sure foundation for our times, a rich store of salvation and wisdom and knowledge." Knowing the Lord and His Word is the key to unlocking this rich storehouse of treasure.

The next two days we will uncover the other powerful weapon God has given us—prayer. Why should we pray? What power lies in prayer? As always, let's go to the source of all wisdom and power…the true Word of God.

Please read each passage. Ask God to open the eyes of your heart so that you will understand what He is saying to you.

1. Luke 11:1: "One day Jesus was praying in a certain place. When he finished, one of his disciples said to him, 'Lord, teach us to pray....'"

   A. What did the disciples see Jesus doing?

   B. What did one of the disciples ask of Jesus?

   C. Do you know how to pray? If you've never asked *Jesus* to teach you how to pray, please take a minute or two right now and earnestly ask Him to teach you. (*This is a personal reflection question. You won't be asked to share this in your group.*)

2. Referring to Jesus, Ephesians 3:12 states, "In Him and through faith in Him we may approach God with freedom and confidence."

   A. In whose name are we to come to God?

   B. How does God allow us to approach Him? Please fill in the blanks.

"In Him and through _____ in Him we may approach God with _____ and _____."

What an awesome privilege to boldly approach God with freedom and confidence! I know I would likely be speechless if I had an audience with the president of the United States. I would be afraid of saying something stupid or meaningless. But God's Word tells me that I can— with confidence—freely go before the Creator of the universe, the One True God! When I approach the Father, my Abba, in the name of His Son, He welcomes me with open arms. I can tell Him whatever is on my heart. I don't have to be afraid of Him or fear His response. He will never ridicule me, disdain me, or sigh with impatience at my coming to Him again and again.

God *implores* us to come to Him. He *wants* us to come to Him!

3. Luke 18:1: "Then Jesus told his disciples a parable to show them that they should always pray and not give up."

A parable is a short story that contains a moral or lesson. It usually compares the familiar to the unfamiliar. A common explanation holds that a parable is "an earthly story with a heavenly meaning." Jesus used many parables to teach his followers spiritual truths.

A. What reason does Luke give for Jesus telling his disciples a parable in Luke 18:1?

B. What do you think it means to persist in prayer?

C. Have you been offering God a prayer recently, but haven't received a clear answer? Why should you "not give up"?

The NIV Life Application Bible explains what it means to persist in prayer. "Always praying means keeping our requests constantly before God as we live for Him day by day, believing He will answer. When we live by faith we are not to give up. God may delay answering, but His delays always have good reason. As we persist in prayer we grow in character, faith, and hope."[30]

4. Lam. 2:19: "Arise, cry out in the night, as the watches of the night begin; pour out your heart like water in the presence of the Lord. Lift up your hands to him for the lives of your children…."

A. Describe how this author implored his readers to pray for their children.

B. What is it about your child that has you crying out in the night? I invite you right now to lift up your hands to the Lord and pour out your heart to Him. He loves you. He loves your child. He is listening.

Are there times when you feel baffled, when you simply don't know how or for what to pray? Listen to God's powerful words of comfort….

---

30 The *Life Application Study Bible,* New International Version edition, (Tyndale House Publishers, 1988, 1989, 1990, 1991), 1842.

5. Rom. 8:26–27, (NLT): Paul writes, "And the Holy Spirit helps us in our weakness. For example, we don't know what God wants us to pray for. But the Holy Spirit prays for us with groanings that cannot be expressed in words. 27 And the Father who knows all hearts knows what the Spirit is saying, for the Spirit pleads for us believers in harmony with God's own will."

    A. Who helps us in our weakness? Write down your answer and then circle it in the passage above.

    B. Who prays for us when we don't know for what we ought to pray? Write down your answer and then circle it in the passage above.

    C. Who pleads for us before the Father in "harmony with God's own will"? Write down your answer and then circle it in the passage above.

The answers to these questions tell us exactly why we can approach God with such confidence! We're not doing this on our own. The very Spirit of God takes our words before the throne of God. He perfects them and pleads before the Father "with groanings" on our behalf. He prays in harmony with God's good and perfect will.

We receive a promise in Proverbs 15:29b: "The Lord…hears the prayer of the righteous." Did you realize that God not only hears our prayers, but that He *never forgets* a prayer we've prayed? Listen to what Pete Greig and Dave Roberts wrote in their book, *Red Moon Rising*. "[God] seemed to say, 'even though you forget most of the prayers you pray to me, I never forget a single thing you ask….' He has treasured every little prayer I've prayed and is still weaving fulfillments. It's a concept almost beyond comprehension; there must be answered prayers most days that I never even recognize as such."[31]

God's own Word testifies to this. In Revelation 5:8 and 8:3–4, we hear that God collects our prayers and considers them as sweet incense to Him! What a transforming thought! God never forgets a prayer. No wonder James could testify with such boldness, "The prayer of a righteous man [or woman] is powerful and effective" (James 5:16)!

6. How did the Lord speak to you today?

---

31 Pete Greig and Dave Roberts; *Red Moon Rising* (Lake Mary, Relevant Books, 2005), 112.

Walking the Journey

This morning I had a "Care Page" update from a friend whose young daughter is struggling with cancer. I appreciate getting the Care Page updates, so that I know how they're doing and how best to pray for them.

This morning my sixteen-year-old son had a serious rage. He was aggressive towards me and towards our dog, and caused damage to our home. Our son, who has bipolar disorder and anxiety disorder, has been very unstable the past few weeks. Each time he melts down and has a rage, my husband and I wonder, "Is this the time he goes to the hospital?"

Mental illness still carries a stigma. Parents don't post Care Page updates on their children who are ill with a mental illness. In fact, too often we feel judged for our poor parenting. We've been told that we allow our son to call all the shots and to manipulate us. Although my husband and I are open with family and friends about our son and the struggles we face daily, we want to protect our son. So we don't publicly post the details of his illness (or publicly ask for prayer in church).

It's easy to feel isolated in this struggle. By the time you figure out that your child is not just a "bad kid" you've already begun to pull back from many social events. It's hard when your child is always the one causing the problems in family and social gatherings. It's easier to just stay home. When our child's illness flares up, life centers on appointments with our family therapist, psychiatrist, the schoolteachers and counselor. We spend a lot of time and energy just trying to keep it all together. The psychiatry road is a difficult road to maneuver. Who can possibly understand the challenges we're faced with?

I know this all sounds bleak. To be honest, there are many times I've asked God to "take this cup from us." But God has been so faithful through it all. He's actively taught us about His love. He's opened our hearts to the marginalized in our society. God has also taught us much about suffering. The way we suffer for our young son is nothing compared to how God suffers for His children. Through our son's illness, we have a taste of what Paul was talking about when he said, "I want to know Christ and the power of His resurrection, and the fellowship of sharing in His suffering…" (Phil. 3:10). God knows exactly what our suffering feels like. He is feeling it, too. My husband and I share a special bond because of what we experience with our son. No one else walks this road with us minute by minute. In this same way, we also share a special bond with our Father. He's holding our hands as He walks this road with us, and we trust Him for our next step.

An article I wrote for a newsletter that deals with disabilities.

WEEK 5, DAY 5

LISTEN AND LEARN...PRAY IN HIS WILL

Yesterday we asked the Lord Jesus to teach us to pray. We know we can boldly come before God's throne with freedom and confidence! We learned that the Holy Spirit intercedes on our behalf. We ended the day with the awe-inspiring thought that God never forgets a single prayer we offer.

Today we will learn what it means to "be still" before the Lord and why this is important. We are also going to scratch the surface of what it means to pray in God's will...and what happens when God seems to say "no."

Please read each passage. Ask God to open the eyes of your heart so that you will understand what He is saying to you.

1. Ps. 46:10: "Be still, and know that I am God;

    I will be exalted among the nations,

    I will be exalted in the earth."

    A. Why does the psalmist tell us to "be still"?

    B. In the midst of a busy day, what creative ways could you find to be still before God?

The Hebrew word for *know* in this verse literally means to comprehend God with our whole being...heart, mind, and soul. In other words, this verse doesn't just speak of head knowledge about who God is. The words imply an intimacy, much as a husband and wife *know* one another. The psalm calls us to experience God's presence, to recognize and understand who He is.

2. Ps. 32:8: "I will instruct you and teach you in the way you should go;

    I will counsel you and watch over you."

The prophet Isaiah wrote, "This is what the LORD says— your Redeemer, the Holy One of Israel: 'I am the LORD your God, who teaches you what is best for you, who directs you in the way you should go'" (Isa. 48:17).

A. How is the Lord depicted in these verses? Choose all that apply.

_____ a task master

_____ a teacher

_____ a counselor

_____ a tyrant

_____ a blind old man

_____ a guide.

B. According to the verse from Isaiah, what is the Lord teaching us?

C. In what parts of your life do you feel the need for some instruction from the Lord, especially in your relationship with your child?

I invite you to turn that need into a prayer. You can pray something like this, *"Lord, You promise in Your word that You will teach me what is best for me. Right now I'm really struggling with _____. I honestly don't know what to do. I'm asking You to guide me. Please direct me in the way I should go. Show me what to do and how to do it. Thank You for watching over me and leading me on Your path. In the name of Jesus, I come, Amen."*

3. Luke 10:39, 41–42: " Martha had a sister called Mary, who sat at the Lord's feet listening to what he said. 41 'Martha, Martha,' the Lord answered, 'you are worried and upset about many things, 42 but only one thing is needed. Mary has chosen what is better, and it will not be taken away from her.'"

A. What are we told that Mary did?

B. How did the Lord describe Martha's attitude? Fill in the blanks. "Martha, Martha…, you are _____ and _____ about many things…"

C. What did Jesus say about Mary's decision to sit at Jesus' feet? Fill in the blanks.

"Mary has chosen what _____, and it will not be _____ _____ from her."

D. What was Mary *doing* as she sat at Jesus' feet?

E. The next time you are "worried and upset about many things," what advice would you think Jesus has for you? How can you follow His advice? List some ways and be prepared to share them with your group.

We can find numerous examples in Scripture that seem to tell us to "name and claim" whatever we desire and it will be ours. So what happens when God says "no" to a prayer? Are we not praying with enough faith? Why doesn't God always answer our sincere and earnest prayers with a *yes*?

These are hard questions, and books have been written on this subject—with many varied answers! Today we'll look at a few examples in Scripture that will entice us to peer a little more closely at God's heart of love for us, and what it means to pray in His will.

4. 1 John 5:14–15, (NLT): John writes, "And we are confident that He hears us whenever we ask for anything that pleases Him. 15 And since we know He hears us when we make our requests, we also know that He will give us what we ask for."

   A. Fill in the blanks: "And we are confident that He hears us whenever we _____ for anything that pleases Him. And since we know He hears us when we _____ our _____, we also know that He will give us what we _____ for."

   B. Using the words you placed in the blanks, answer a question: what does God invite us to do?

   C. What can we believe with confidence when we make our requests to God? (See 1 John 5:14.)

   D. When we approach God with a request, whose will ought we be seeking? Underline the phrase in 1 John 5:14 that highlights this reminder.

This verse emphasizes *God's will*, not our own will. When we line up our prayers and petitions with God's will, He promises to hear us and answer our prayer. It's important to remember that our thoughts are not necessarily God's thoughts, nor is our timing necessarily God's timing.

5. Isa. 55:8–9: "For My thoughts are not your thoughts, neither are your ways My ways," declares the LORD. 9 "As the heavens are higher than the earth, so are My ways higher than your ways and My thoughts than your thoughts."

   A. Who is the speaker in the passage?

   B. Let's personalize this passage. Repeat this passage to the Lord as a reminder and an affirmation that His ways and thoughts are higher than ours. Fill in the blanks with either your name (or personal pronoun) or God's name.

   "For ____ thoughts are not ____ thoughts, neither are ____ ways ____ ways, declares the Lord. As the heavens are higher than the earth, so are ____ ways higher than ____ ways and ____ thoughts than ____ thoughts."

6. In Day 1, Week 5, we studied John 10:10: "The thief comes only to steal, kill, and destroy; I have come that they may have life, and have it to the full."

   A. What does Satan come to do?

B. What would Satan love to do with your faith?

C. Satan not only is a thief and murderer, he is also a liar. Listen to Jesus' harsh words in John 8:44. "[Satan] was a murderer from the beginning, not holding to the truth, for there is no truth in him. When he lies, he speaks his native language, for he is a liar and the father of lies."

   1. Fill in the blanks. "He was a _____ from the beginning, not holding to the truth, for there is _____ _____ in him. When he lies, he speaks his native language, for he is a _____ and the father of lies."

   2. What is Satan's "native language"?

From the beginning, Satan was both a murderer and a liar. When we go all the way back to Genesis 3 (the account of the fall of humanity), we see that Satan twisted God's words when he tempted Eve. He said, "Did God *really* say…?"

Satan has always planned to create doubt and confusion in our minds about God's absolute *goodness*. One way he does this is to entice us to doubt God's goodness and love for us whenever God does not give the answers to our prayers that we seek. Satan boldly points an accusing finger at God and tells us that every "no" from God is just another example of how He really doesn't love us. He whispers to us, "Did God *really* say…?"

What about Jesus? Did Jesus get a "yes" to every prayer He prayed? The heart-wrenching scene in the Garden of Gethsemane reminds us powerfully that even Jesus submitted to the greater will of His Father. Jesus' flesh was crying out, "No, don't make me do this." But He obediently submitted His flesh and His humanity to the Father.

Oh, how important it is for us to believe that anytime we are given a "no" from God, it is *always* for a greater "yes"!

When we listen to Jesus as Mary did, sitting quietly and attentively at His feet, we will intimately come to *know* our Savior. We will learn much about the will of Jesus for our lives. We will learn that *our* will is not necessarily *His* will. As we come to know our Creator more personally and as we mature in our faith, our prayers and petitions will come to align more completely with God's will. Jesus Himself always prayed with God's interests in mind. We will see incredible answers to prayer—and experience greater peace—when we begin to discuss with God what *He* wants for us, instead of demanding from Him what *we* want for ourselves. When we align our prayers to His will, praying in unity with Him, He will listen and He will answer. Let's start praying with confidence!

7. How did the Lord speak to you today?

WALKING THE JOURNEY

Jesus is Enough (A Prayer from Psalm 131)[32]

To pray *Jesus is Enough* meditatively, you need to pray it s-l-o-w-l-y. Offer this prayer one line at a time, letting the last word or image of each line echo throughout your soul as you pause quietly before going onto the next line. At the end when you pray only the name of Jesus, simply remain in stillness with your Lord, letting Jesus hold you….

Jesus is enough for me to keep my soul tranquil and quiet like a child in its mother's arms—content…

Jesus is enough for me to keep my soul tranquil and quiet like a child in its mother's arms…

Jesus is enough for me to keep my soul tranquil and quiet…

Jesus is enough for me to keep my soul tranquil…

Jesus is enough for me to keep my soul…

Jesus is enough for me to keep…

Jesus is enough for me…

Jesus' smile is enough…

Jesus' embrace is enough…

Jesus' breath is enough…

Jesus is enough…

Jesus…

---

32 Bill Gaultiere, *Jesus is Enough for Me!*, "Christian Soul Care Devotional," www.soulshepherding.org. Used with permission.

AFTERWORD...

"He will be the sure foundation for your times, a rich store of salvation and wisdom and knowledge; the fear of the Lord is the key to this treasure." (Isa. 33:6)

Thank you for taking this journey with me to the heart of God. My prayer is that you found encouragement and received new hope along the way. God has specifically chosen you and equipped you to be your child's mother. His anointing rests on you! God promises to give you His divine power to live an abundant life today. When you're faced with more challenges and discouragements than you think you're able to withstand, remember that God has given you *everything you need for life and godliness.* Tap into His mighty power.

How will we truly know God, recognize His voice, or understand what He wants to teach us if we never sit still long enough to hear? Like Mary, we need to quiet ourselves and sit at His feet, drinking deeply from the Living Water. *Be still and know that I am God.*

Never forget that you were appointed by God to be the mom of a very special child. You prayed for this child before he or she was born, and God has answered your prayers. His blessing rests on you. You can do this, no matter how difficult the task. His power is available to you; He has a storehouse of wisdom and knowledge that He's waiting to open up for your benefit. *The fear of the Lord is the key to this treasure.*

I'm praying for you as you walk this difficult road. Even though I don't see you or even know you, God does. He knows your name; He knows your needs; He knows your heart. He loves you and under His wings you will find refuge, strength, and healing. *"The Sun of Righteousness will rise with healing in His wings"* (Mal. 4:2).

Bev Roozeboom